THE WAY OF ST JAMES
SPAIN

THE MAJOR PILGRIM ROUTES THROUGH FRANCE AND SPAIN

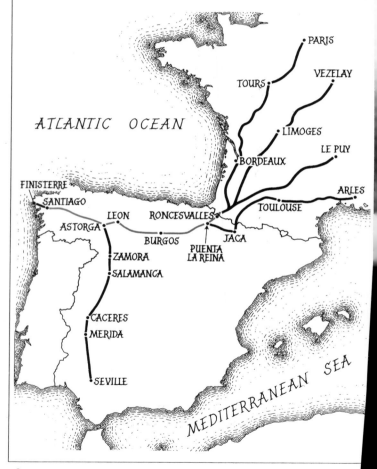

THE WAY OF SAINT JAMES SPAIN

by
Alison Raju

CICERONE PRESS
MILNTHORPE, CUMBRIA

© Alison Raju 1994
ISBN 1 85284 142 7

A catalogue record for this book is available from the British Library

for Jim

I would like to thank Fernando Ruiz Chavarri of Logroño and
Luis Manuel Fernández Vázquez of Montforte de Lemos (Lugo)
for their assistance.

Colour photographs by Dr Patrick Hurley
Maps by Martin Collins

Advice to Readers

Readers are advised that whilst every effort is taken by the author to
ensure the accuracy of this guidebook, changes can occur which may
affect the contents. It is advisable to check locally on transport,
accommodation, shops etc but even rights-of-way can be altered and,
more especially overseas, paths can be eradicated by landslip, forest
fires or changes of ownership.

The publisher would welcome notes of any such changes

Front Cover: The symbol of St James near El Burgo Ranero

CONTENTS

Pinman Waymark

Introduction

The Way of Saint James is a long-distance footpath with a difference. People have been walking it - as a pilgrimage route - for over a thousand years and in 1987 it became the first European Cultural Itinerary. Its 709 kilometres from the Spanish monastery at Roncesvalles in the foothills of the Pyrenees to Santiago de Compostela in the western reaches of Galicia have changed little in all that time. For although sections of it have now become modern tarred roads and many of the "hospitals" and other accommodation set up by religious orders along the way to minister to the needs of pilgrims have long since disappeared, the "camino", as it is known in Spain, still passes through the same villages, crosses the same rivers, visits the same chapels, churches, cathedrals and other monuments as did the path taken by our predecessors in centuries gone by.

The Way of Saint James is also a long-distance footpath with a difference in that the vast majority of those who walk it are not experienced walkers at all. Many have never done any serious walking in their lives and many will never do any again, for here, as in the past, walking is a means of transport, a means to an end, rather than an activity for its own sake. Most long-distance footpaths also avoid not only large towns but even quite small villages as well; the Way of Saint James, on the other hand, because of its historic origins and the need for shelter, deliberately seeks them out. Several thousand people walk the Way every year, whether from the Pyrenees, from different parts of France or from even further afield: it is not uncommon, even nowadays, to meet Swiss, German, Belgian or Dutch pilgrims, for example, who have set out from home to make the entire journey on foot. However, one of the differences between the modern pilgrim and his historical counterpart, whether he walks, goes by bicycle or on horseback, is that few, if any, return home by the same means of transport. The modern pilgrim route has become a "one-way street" and it is rare, today, to encounter anyone with either enough time or the inclination to return to his or her point of departure by the same means as he

7

or she set out.

People make the journey to Santiago for a variety of reasons - historical, cultural, religious, as a significant action or event in their lives - and it is something that many Spaniards in particular think of doing at least once in their lifetime, even if they do not actually manage to. Modern pilgrims are people of all ages and walks of life, probably the majority from Spain, but with a great many each year from France, Switzerland, Belgium, Holland and Germany. (In contrast there are very few from Britain at present.) Many travel alone, many in twos and threes, many in quite large groups, particularly those on foot. Many complete the entire journey in one stretch; others, with more limited time, cover a section at a time over several years. Most who have walked the camino would probably agree afterwards, however, that it has changed their lives in some way, even though they may never have set out with this intention at all.

This book is intended both as a companion volume to Hal Bishop's guide to the French section of the Way of Saint James from Le Puy to the Pyrenees (Cicerone Press, 1989) and as a guide in its own right to the Spanish part of the walk. It begins in Roncesvalles (Roncevaux in French) but for those who would prefer to start in Saint Jean-Pied-de-Port, either because they would like to cross the Pyrenees on foot or because they find it more convenient to travel there from Britain (rather than going to Pamplona and then backtracking), details of this stage are given in the Appendices. Likewise, for those who feel that their journey would be incomplete unless they continued to Finisterre, a description of this route is also given at the end. These are followed by an outline guide to the Vía de la Plata (see next section) and a glossary of geographical and other frequently encountered terms. A list of suggestions for further reading is given in the Bibliography.

The walk can be completed in a month by anyone who is fairly fit and also likes to visit places of interest along the way. It can be undertaken in sections, too, by those who lack the time to do it all in one go or who would just like to cover certain stages. Anyone in Britain who is thinking of walking, cycling or riding any part of the route should certainly consider contacting the Confraternity of Saint James for advice and membership - their annually updated guides to accommodation and other facilities are extremely useful (see the last page of the book for address). Most parts of the walker's route are also accessible to those riding mountain (though not touring) bikes.

HISTORY

Pilgrims have been travelling to Santiago de Compostela on foot or on horseback (and more recently by bicycle) for over a thousand years. (The Bishop of Le Puy, who went there in AD950, was one of the first.) At the height of its popularity in the eleventh and twelfth centuries over half a million people a year are said to have made the pilgrimage from different parts of Europe, the majority of them from France.

Pilgrimages had been popular amongst Christians ever since Constantine the Great had the Church of the Holy Sepulchre built over the site of Christ's burial in Jerusalem, in AD326, and the discovery, shortly afterwards, of the Holy Cross itself. Rome, the burial place of Saint Peter, was the other great centre of Christian pilgrimage in the Middle Ages, along with Santiago de Compostela after the finding of the remains of Saint James the Great (son of Zebedee, brother of John and Christ's cousin). The high point of this third pilgrimage occurred between the years 1000 and 1500 but although numbers dwindled after that, due to the Reformation and other, political, factors, the stream of pilgrims making the trudge westwards to the far reaches of Galicia in north-west Spain never completely dried up and in the late twentieth century is making something of a comeback. The Cathedral authorities in Santiago maintain a register of pilgrims and in 1991 recorded a total of 7274 travelling on foot, bicycle or horseback (compared with 5760 in 1989, the year of the Pope's August visit there, and 4918 in 1990).

Legend

After the death of Christ the disciples dispersed to different parts of the then known world, to spread the Gospel as they had been bidden. Saint James went to Spain, we are told, where he spent a couple of years evangelising, though apparently without a great deal of success. He then returned to Jerusalem but was beheaded by Herod shortly afterwards, in AD44. Immediately following his martyrdom, however, his followers are said to have taken his body to Jaffa, on the coast, where a ship was miraculously waiting for them and they set off back to Spain. They landed in Iria Flavia on the coast of Galicia, present-day Padrón, some twenty kilometres from what is now Santiago de Compostela, after a journey (and in a stone boat!) which is purported to have taken only a week, thereby providing proof of angelic assistance. Saint James's body was then buried in a tomb on a hillside, along with, later on, two of his followers, and then forgotten for the next 750 years. The story is considerably more complicated than this but these are the bare bones.

Early in the ninth century Pelagius, a hermit living in that part of Spain, had a vision (which he subsequently reported to Theodomir, bishop of Ira Flavia) in which he saw a very large bright star, surrounded by a ring of smaller ones, shining over a deserted spot in the hills. The matter was investigated and a tomb found there containing three bodies. They were immediately identified as those of Saint James and two of his followers and when Alfonso II, King of the Asturias (791-824), went there he declared Saint James the patron saint of Spain. He built a church and a small monastery over the tomb in the saint's honour, around which a town grew up. It was known as campus de la stella or campus stellae, later shortened to compostela. This is one explanation of the origin of the name. Another is that it derives from the Latin componere (to bury), as a Roman cemetery or early Christian necropolis is known to have existed under the site of the present-day cathedral in Santiago - and where the remains of Saint James are still believed to be housed today.

The pilgrimage

News of the discovery soon spread. It was encouraged to do so, moreover, both by Archbishop Gelmírez and the cathedral authorities, who were anxious to promote the town as a pilgrimage centre, thus attracting money to the area, and by the monks of Cluny, who saw in it the opportunity to assist the Spanish church in their long struggle against the Moors. Both factions were also helped by the fact that the Turks had seized the Holy Sepulchre in 1078, thus putting a stop to pilgrimages to Jerusalem. However,

Santiago was attractive as a potential pilgrim "venue" in other respects too, as it fulfilled the various criteria necessary to make a pilgrimage there worthy of merit. It was far away (from most parts of France, for example) and difficult to reach, thus requiring a good deal of hardship and endurance to get there (and back again too, of course). It was sufficiently dangerous (wolves, bandits, fever, rivers that were difficult to cross, unscrupulous ferrymen) as well as being in Spain, then locked tight in struggle with the Moors, and for this reason many pilgrims travelled in quite large groups. (A considerable corpus of songs of pilgrims from previous centuries still exists, sung as they walked along.)

The road itself was also well supplied with shrines, relics and other sights worth seeing. As traffic increased roads, bridges and hospices were built and the pilgrimage churches, characterised by their ambulatories round the inside of the building in order to facilitate viewing of the relics exposed behind the high altar, were endowed with a growing number of such items, thus ensuring that pilgrims would pass that way to see them. Many churches were dedicated to Saint James and many more contain his statue, whether as a pilgrim (Santiago peregrino) or as the Moor-slayer (Santiago matamoros). A considerable number of very tiny chapels or ermitas dedicated to San Roque, the pilgrim saint from Montpellier, were also built along the way. (After a pilgrimage to Rome San Roque devoted his life to caring for plague victims but withdrew to live in a forest when he contracted a disease which left him with an unsightly sore on his left thigh. For this reason he is depicted in art with the front flap of his coat turned back, to warn people to keep away from him, and is accompanied by the faithful dog who brought the saint his daily rations, often with a loaf of bread in his mouth.)

Why did people go on pilgrimages anyway, though? For a variety of reasons. As a profession of faith, as a form of punishment (a system of fixed penalties for certain crimes/sins was in operation during the Middle Ages), as a means of atonement, as a way of acquiring merit (and thus, for example, reducing or, in certain cases, cutting in half, the amount of time spent in Purgatory) and as an opportunity to venerate the relics of the many saints available along the principal routes to Santiago. (Indulgences were available to those who visited shrines.) No doubt, too, there were some who were just glad of the opportunity to escape their surroundings and later there were professional pilgrims who would (for a fee) undertake to do the pilgrimage on behalf of someone else who could afford the money but not the time to do it him or herself. Those with the means to do so went on horseback and some wealthy people made the pilgrimage along with a considerable retinue. The majority of pilgrims went on foot, however, and even amongst the rich there were some who preferred to walk, rather than ride, because of the greater "merit" they would attain afterwards.

The pilgrim in former times was not at all sure that he would eventually reach his destination, let alone return home in one piece, so before setting out he took leave of his family and employer, made his will and generally put his affairs in order. He (or she) obtained his credentials (pilgrim passport) from his bishop or church, which he could then present in order to obtain food and lodging in the many pilgrim "hospitals" and other establishments along the way. This was both a precaution against the growing number of "coquillards" or pseudo-pilgrims and as a means of providing proof of his journey: he had his papers stamped at different stages along the way so that once he arrived in Santiago he could obtain his Compostela or certificate of pilgrimage from the Cathedral authorities there. This in turn entitled him to stay in the pilgrim shelters on his return journey as well as furnishing evidence, if needed, that he had actually made the pilgrimage successfully.

The pilgrim had his staff and scrip blessed in church before setting out and travelled light, carrying little else but a gourd for water and his scallop shell. This singled him out as a pilgrim, rather than as any other type of traveller, and is the symbol embedded above doorways and in other places on the many and varied buildings that accommodated him along the different pilgrim's roads. There are different explanations as to the origins of the "coquille Saint Jacques" but one is that when the followers of Saint James arrived in the port of Iria Flavia with the apostle's body they saw a man riding along the beach (a bridegroom in some versions) whose horse took fright and then plunged into the sea. When they re-emerged both horse and rider were covered from head to foot in scallop shells (and even today the beaches in this part of Galicia are strewn with them). It was customary to set out in the springtime in order to reach Santiago for the feast of Saint James on July 25th and return home for the winter. This was especially true in Holy Years, those in which July 25th falls on a Sunday (the next one is in 1999), the only time the "Puerta Santa" or Holy Door of the Cathedral of Santiago is open. This is sealed up at the end of each such year and then symbolically broken down again by the Archbishop in a special ceremony in the evening of December 31st preceding the new Holy year, a year during which special concessions and indulgences were, and still are, available to pilgrims. On returning home many joined confraternities of former pilgrims in their own countries, the forerunners of the modern-day associations of "Friends of Saint James" that now exist in several European countries to support, promote and encourage the different routes to Santiago.

Many pilgrims wrote accounts of their experiences but as early as the twelfth century the first real "travel guide" was produced, probably between 1140 and 1150. Its author was for a long time believed to be one Aimery Picaud, a cleric from Parthenay-le-Vieux in the Poitou region of France, and it formed part of a Latin manuscript known as the *Codex Calixtinus*. However, instead of relating the journey of one particular individual this was intended as a guide for the use of prospective pilgrims (especially French). It describes the four roads through France (see below) and divides the route from the Pyrenees to Santiago into thirteen (somewhat unequal) stages. It lists, with comments, the places through which the Camino francés passes, indicates some of the hazards pilgrims may encounter and contains advice on the good and bad rivers along the way, indicating which are safe to drink and which should be avoided. The author also describes in some detail the inhabitants of the different regions through which the prospective pilgrim will pass, their language (including one of the earliest lists of Basque words), customs and characteristics, none of which compare at all favourably, in his opinion, with those of the people of his native Poitou. He includes a list of shrines to be visited along the different roads through France, a description of the city of Santiago and its churches and a detailed account of the cathedral's history, architecture and canons. It is now thought that this guide was not, in fact, written by one person but was a compilation designed, under the influence of the energetic Bishop Diego Gelmírez, to promote Santiago de Compostela as a pilgrimage centre. Regardless of its authorship, this guide once attributed to Aymery Picaud was certainly instrumental in popularising the itineraries of the four main pilgrim roads through France and the Camino francés in Spain. It has recently been translated into English: see bibliography.

Routes to Santiago

Although the name Camino de Santiago has become synonymous with the Camino francés or "French Road", the route described in this book is not the one and only Way of Saint James. In former times, when pilgrims made their way to Santiago from many different places, several well-established routes grew up (see map). In France, for example, there were four main departure points. The route from Paris, the *Via Turonensis*, passed through Orléans, Tours, Poitiers, Bordeaux and Dax. From Vézelay pilgrims took the *Via Lemovicensis* through Limoges, Périgeux, Bazas and Mont-de-Marsan while those from Le Puy took the *Via Podensis* and passed through Conques, Cahors, Moissac, Aire-sur-l'Adour and Navarrenx. All three routes joined up near Ostabat on the French side of the Pyrenees, to continue over the mountains to Roncesvalles and on across the north of Spain as the Camino francés. The fourth road, from Arles, known as the *Via Tolosana*, visited Saint-Gilles du Gard, Toulouse, Auch and Oloron but crossed the Pyrenees further east at the Col de Somport, from where it is known as the Camino aragonés, before merging with the other three at Puenta la Reina.

Other important routes included the northern one along the Costa Cantabrica on the north coast of Spain, passing through Hernani, Zumaya, Guernica, Bilbao, Lareda and Casteñada before turning inland to reach Santiago via Oviedo and Lugo. This was the path taken by many English pilgrims, who went by ship as far as Bordeaux and then continued on foot, whilst others sailed to La Coruña and then walked the rest of the way along one of the Rutas del Mar, one of which was known as the Camino inglés. The Vía de la Plata or Camino mozárabe, on the other hand, was the way taken by pilgrims from the south of Spain once it had been reconquered from the Moors, passing through Seville, Mérida, Cáceres, Salamanca and Zamora before joining the Camino francés at Astorga. An outline guide to this route - fully waymarked today - is given in Appendix C. There were also routes from the east coast of Spain as well as two <u>caminos</u>, south to north, through Portugal, one inland, the other along the coast. The Way of Saint James described here therefore corresponds to the one known as the <u>Camino francés</u>, the most widely-used and best-documented of the many pilgrim roads to Santiago; it begins in Roncesvalles and passes through Pamplona, Estella, Logroño, Burgos, Sahagún, León, Astorga, Ponferrada, Villafranca del Bierzo and Sarria.

TOPOGRAPHY, ECONOMY AND LANGUAGE

The <u>Camino francés</u> begins in the Basque country, whether you start on the French or the Spanish side of the Pyrenees. Roncesvalles is in Navarre (and not in one of the three provinces making up the autonomous <u>región</u> of the País Vasco), but a great deal of Basque influence is evident, for example in local architecture. On both sides of the Pyrenees the large Basque houses with overhanging eaves, often ornately decorated, outside staircases and balconies running the whole length of one or more sides of the building are common, as is also the <u>frontón</u> or pelota court, to be found in almost every village of any size. The Basque language (<u>Euskerra</u> in Basque, <u>Vascuence</u> in Castilian) is unrelated to any of the Romance languages and its origins are still the subject of scholarly debate. It is an official language in the four Basque provinces, alongside Castilian, and is much in evidence in Navarre, whether in ordinary conversation, on television (in bars, for example), on signs, notices and place name boards.

After the high mountains and deep valleys of the Pyrenees, where sheep are a common sight, the landscape changes, flattening out to become more undulating as the <u>camino</u> makes its way down to Pampelona, a fortress town set up on a hill in the middle of a wide, fertile plain. It also gets hotter and dustier in summer, when it rarely rains, and the older vernacular houses are brown, built in adobe with red pantile roofs. This area has much in common with the landscape of Castille-León, though you remain in Navarre until the outskirts of Logroño.

La Rioja, like Navarre, is both a province and an autonomous

15

región (Spain is divided into seventeen of the latter, each containing one or several provincias) and is well known for its excellent wines. It is also characterised by a deep red clay soil, contrasting sharply with the golden corn in summer, the bright blue of the sky and the dark green of many of the trees, particularly in the early morning and evening light, and you will come across a number of potteries or alfarerías, especially in the section between Logroño and Nájera. From here to Burgos, before it climbs up into the woods in the Montes de Oca, the camino continues its way through undulating countryside where you will encounter, in common with many other parts of Spain, large flocks of sheep and goats, often on the move with their shepherds and goatherds, in search of new grazing on cornfields that have just been harvested.

As you continue into Castille-León, one of the largest of the autonomous regions (with nine provinces), you will meet the first of a special type of local inhabitant: the cigüeña. The ubiquitous stork has a nest (sometimes as many as three or four) on the tower of nearly every church and is a characteristic sight in this part of Spain, as are also the seemingly endless cornfields. After Burgos the camino wends its way up onto the meseta, the high plateau or table land where the walker often has the feeling of being on the "roof of the world", after which it descends through the rolling countryside of the province of Palencia into the flat plains of León where several places include the suffix "del Páramo" (bleak plateau/plain) in their names. (Other places along the Way of Saint James end in "del Camino", evidence of the route the pilgrims took in former times.)

After Astorga the camino enters the Montes de León, slowly, at first, through the area known as the Maragatería. There are different theories as to the origins of the people in this area, who have their own distinctive customs, traditions and music, one of which is that, because of their isolated situation, they are the descendants of a very ancient race who escaped the effects of successive invasions. There are many abandoned or semi-abandoned villages in this section, although some are now coming to life again, due, in part, to the revival of interest in the Camino de Santiago. An example of a typical maragato village, now a National Monument and worth a short detour, is Castrillo de los Polvares, just off the route beyond Astorga. After the Cruz de Fierro the camino enters the mountainous

The octagonal Romanesque church at Eunate is a pilgrims' burial place connected with the Order of St John of Jerusalem
The 11th century bridge at Puente la Reina, attributed to Dona Mayor, wife of Sancho the Greater of Navarre

The town of Logrono with its bridge over the River Ebro
A fountain by the cathedral at Burgos. The man is retrieving coins from the
water

area of El Bierzo with its fertile valleys and excellent wines, though the latter are not yet as internationally well known as those of La Rioja.

After Vega de Valcarce, still, in fact, in the province of León but totally different from the landscape where the <u>camino</u> enters it 7km before Sahagún, the pilgrim road climbs up and up, through chestnut woods and then out into open country up to El Cebreiro at 1,300m, shortly before which it enters Galicia. From here the route changes dramatically in character.

Galicia is the autonomous <u>región</u> comprising the provinces of Lugo, Orense, Pontevedra and La Coruña. It has its own language (not a dialect), related to Portuguese, and which, together with <u>castellano</u> (ie. "Spanish") is used as an official language in the region. As a result you will find that not only will people reply to you in <u>gallego</u> but that all road signs, official notices etc. appear in both languages. The spelling of place names often varies between the two languages and as at present the <u>castellano</u> forms have not yet been officially standardised the names you see on maps and notices may differ from those on signposts and on entry to villages big enough to have place name boards. Some of the more common variants are the interchange of "b" and "v" (as in Valos/Balos, for example), "o" and "ou" and "e" and "ei".

Galicia is a very green, lush area for the most part, with the highest rainfall in Spain. Unlike the south of Spain with its enormous <u>latifundios</u> (very large properties) the land in Galicia is divided (and subdivided) into tiny, often uneconomic individual holdings (<u>minifundios</u>), the result of centuries of sharing out land between its owner's descendants.

As a result you will frequently see people (many of whom are women) working in the fields doing tasks by hand that would elsewhere be done more economically by machine. Unlike parts of Navarre and Castille-León, too, where villages are often very far apart but whose buildings are tightly concentrated together, those in Galicia are often tiny, not far from each other and much more spread out so that you are not usually very far from a building of some kind. The region is also criss-crossed with a veritable maze of old green lanes, which wend their way through fields separated from each other with stone boundaries made of large slabs set on end like rows of giant teeth, so that without some kind of waymarking system the camino would be almost impossible to follow. Another characteristic feature of the Galician countryside is the <u>horreo</u>: a long rectangular granary, of stone, or sometimes brick, raised up on pillars and used for storing potatoes and corncobs. They have slightly pitched roofs with a cross at one end, a decorative knob at the other. <u>Horreos</u> vary greatly in length, from those that are only three or four metres long to enormous structures, with two or three compartments, that stretch for twenty or thirty metres.

Due to its location Galicia remained isolated from the influence of much of what was happening to the rest of Spain in former centuries and as a result still retains evidence of its Celtic origins. The <u>palloza,</u> a round stone dwelling with a thatched roof, dates from these times and several are to be found in the village of El Cebreiro, while traditional Galician music uses the <u>gaita</u> (bagpipe). (Those interested in the architecture, working life and customs of Galicia should visit the Museo do Pobo Galego when they reach Santiago.)

Galicia is also a very heavily wooded area, many of the trees centuries old, and as a result is very pleasant to walk in, even in the height of summer. Unfortunately, however, in recent years, large areas of its forests have been devastated by an epidemic of huge fires, suspected to have been started deliberately but quite why or by whom no one really seems to know. Those who continue on to Finisterre will also see something of the Galician coastline, with its <u>rías,</u> the fjord-like inlets along the Atlantic from the border of Portugal to the province of Asturias on the Costa Verde.

BEFORE YOU GO

a) Read up as much as you can about the Way, it's history, art, architecture and geography, as well as other people's accounts of their journeys. A short bibliography is given at the end of this book.

b) If you are one of the many people walking the Way not already used to walking or aren't used to carrying a rucksack day-in day-out get in plenty of practice before you go. Consider joining your local rambling club at least six months in advance and go out with them as often as you possibly can. Most clubs have walks of different lengths and speeds so you can start with a shorter, slower one if you need to and gradually build up your speed and stamina. The advantages of this are that you can walk with other people, walk in the countryside, have someone to lead who knows the way and suitable places to walk (which you may not) and you can also practise walking in hilly places (which you will need). Then - start increasing the amount of weight and luggage you take out with you until you can carry what you need. After that - go out walking on at least two days in a row on several occasions, in hilly places, carrying all your proposed gear with you: it's a very different matter walking twenty miles on a "one-off" basis from getting up again the following morning, probably stiff and possibly footsore, and starting out all over again. In this way you should have an enjoyable journey, with troublefree feet and back.

c) Don't expect <u>anybody</u> - anybody at all - to speak English! Assume you will have to speak Spanish all the time, for everything you need, however complicated. So, if you are not already fairly fluent, consider a year's evening classes or home study with tapes in your preparations: you will find yourself extremely isolated - and a month is a long time - if you are able merely to carry out practical transactions but are also unable to converse with the (very many) Spanish pilgrims and other people you will meet along the Way.

d) Decide what type of footwear you will be taking - walking shoes, lightweight boots, heavy (thick-soled) trainers, etc., and break them in <u>before</u> you go.

PLANNING YOUR SCHEDULE

Roncesvalles to Santiago can be walked comfortably in a month by anyone who is fairly fit, leaving time to visit places of interest along the Way. Allow plenty of time when planning your itinerary, though, especially if you are not an experienced walker. Start with fairly short stages and always stop <u>before</u> you are tired. You can increase the distances as you get fitter and into the swing of things.

Try not to plan too tight a schedule but allow plenty of time and flexibility to account for unforeseen circumstances (pleasant or otherwise). Where and how many rest days you take is up to you (though Burgos and León are "musts"), as is also whether you include several short days' walking in your programme, arriving at your destination during the late morning so as to have the remainder of the day completely free. If you are having trouble with your feet, though, a complete day off works wonders and is well worth the seeming disruption to your schedule that it might initially seem to be. Allow at least three days to visit Santiago at the end - there is plenty to see and you will also meet up with many of the other walkers you have met along the Way.

EQUIPMENT

1. <u>Rucksack</u>. At least 50 litres if carrying a sleeping bag.
2. <u>Footwear</u> - both to walk in and a spare pair of lightweight trainers/espadrilles/sandals etc.
3. <u>Waterproofs</u>. Even in summer it may rain, especially in Galicia. A "poncho" (ie. cape with a hood and space inside for a rucksack) is far more useful (and far less hot) than a cagoule or anorak.
4. <u>Pullover</u>. Much of the route is high up and it can get cold at night, even in summer.
5. <u>First aid kit</u> (including a needle for draining blisters). The type of elastoplast sold by the metre is more useful than individual dressings. Scissors.
6. <u>Torch</u>, with spare batteries and bulb.
7. <u>Large water bottle</u>. At least two litres if walking in July and August.
8. <u>Sleeping bag</u>. Essential if staying in refugios.
9. <u>Sleeping mat</u>. Useful if staying in refugios, where you may have to sleep on the floor.
10. <u>Stick</u>. Useful for fending off/frightening dogs.
11. <u>Guidebook</u>.
12. <u>Maps</u>.
13. <u>Compass</u>.
14. <u>Whistle</u>.
15. <u>Sun hat</u> (preferably with wide brim).
16. <u>Small dictionary</u>.
17. <u>Mug, spoon and knife</u>.
18. If you are addicted to tea/coffee or can't get going in the

morning without a hot drink a camping gaz type <u>stove</u> is a great advantage, even though it will add extra weight to your luggage. This is especially useful in summer when you will probably set out very early - 5.30 or 6am - to avoid the heat, since cafés and bars rarely open before 8.30 or 9 o'clock. Very few refugios have cooking facilities. (If you do take a camping gaz stove make sure it uses the 200 gram cylinders - smaller ones are not available in Spain). To economise on weight/space take a tin mug both to heat water in and drink out of.

A tent is not worth the trouble as rooms are usually available (eg. in bars, cafés) if you are not staying in refugios.

THERE AND BACK

a) How to get there

<u>Roncesvalles</u>: by bus from Pamplona bus station to Burguete (not Sundays) and then walk the remaining 3km.

<u>Pamplona</u>: by train or coach from Madrid.

<u>Madrid</u>: by air direct from London; by train from London via Paris; by coach direct from London.

<u>Saint Jean-Pied-de-Port</u>: by train from Paris to Bayonne by TGV and then by local train.

<u>Other places along the Way</u> (for those who are only doing a section): Logroño, Burgos, León, and Astorga can all be reached by train from Madrid though the coach may often be both quicker and more convenient. Burgos is also on the London-Madrid coach and the Paris-Madrid train routes.

b) How to get back from Santiago

<u>air</u>: there are scheduled Iberia flights from Santiago to Heathrow. Otherwise go to Madrid by coach or train and fly from there.

<u>train</u>: to Paris. Leaves at 9am everyday, arriving Hendaye late evening, in time for the connection overnight for Paris, arriving early the following morning.

<u>coach</u>: to Paris, direct, 2 to 3 times a week, depending on the time of year. Cheaper, comfortable and slightly shorter than the train journey. Leaves at 1.30pm and arrives 24 hours later (Porte de Charenton). There is also a weekly service direct to London.

BEING THERE

a) Accommodation

Various types of accommodation are available along the Way, ranging from luxurious five-star hotels (such as the state-run <u>Paradores</u> established in redundant historic buildings) down to very basic "refugios" set up in schools and church halls.

"Hotel" usually implies a higher standard of accommodation than that found in a "hostal" which, in turn, normally offers more facilities than a "fonda" ("hospedaje" in Galicia) and, going down the scale, a "posada". ("Residencia" after either a hotel or a hostal means it only provides accommodation: neither meals nor breakfast are available.) A number of bars also provide rooms ("habitaciones" - "camas" means "beds"), so it is worth asking about these, even if there isn't actually a sign or notice to say so. However, a word of warning if you intend to stay in any of these and want to leave early in the morning to avoid walking in the heat: make sure you arrange to pay the previous evening and retain your passport as well as checking, too, how you will actually get out of the building the following morning (ie. which doors or entrances will be locked and how they can be opened). Otherwise you may find yourself unable to leave until at least 9 o'clock.

A "refugio" is simple accommodation set up especially for pilgrims on foot or by bicycle (but not for those accompanied by a back-up vehicle) and is only for those holding a "credencial" or "pilgrim passport" (see below). (This is to ensure that these facilities are not used by "pseudo-pilgrims", hitch-hikers or other travellers.) Refugios are provided by churches, religious orders and "ayuntamientos" (town halls or local authorities). They are being set up in more and more places along the Way, especially since 1989, when the Pope visited Santiago and literally thousands of people made the pilgrimage, either individually or in (sometimes huge) groups and in Galicia in particular, in preparation for the very large numbers expected each Holy Year. Over 80,000 pilgrims received their Compostelas in 1993. Some are in large towns, others in small villages, many are unmanned while others, increasingly, have volunteer wardens during the summer months. The facilities offered vary enormously, from those with beds/bunks, a kitchen and hot showers down to those with only a cold tap and in which you will have to sleep on the floor without a mattress. Some are very large, others very small and in July and August in particular they may be extremely crowded since no one ever seems to be turned away.

Many are still free of charge but you should always offer to pay and there is usually a box for donations towards their upkeep, especially those run by religious or charitable bodies, such as the really excellent "five-star" refugio in Santo Domingo de la Calzada. However, since the availability of these facilities vary greatly from year to year details have not been given here; it is advisable to join the Confraternity of Saint James and obtain their annually revised *Pilgrim Guide to Spain* containing up-to-date information not only on these but all other types of accommodation as well. Unlike hotels, fondas, etc., though, you will not normally encounter any difficulty in leaving refugios early and will find that most other people are doing the same.

b) Planning the day

Long-distance walkers in Britain usually operate on a nine-to-five basis, leaving their accommodation shortly after breakfast and returning in time for an early evening meal. Places of historical, religious or cultural interest directly on the path, such as churches, cathedrals or stately homes that require a detailed indoor visit (as opposed to historic bridges, fortifications, market crosses and so on that can be inspected fairly quickly from the outside) normally work "nine-to-five" as well so that combining walking and sightseeing is usually incompatible. Walkers, in the main, tend just to walk (in Britain). In Spain, however, along the Way of Saint James, not only are there an enormous number of places well worth visiting, of outstanding artistic, architectural, cultural or religious interest, but they are also open at convenient times for the walker: as well as 10am to 1pm in the mornings they normally open again in the evenings from 5pm to 8pm. Churches in small villages are nearly always locked, however, unless there is a service going on, although it is often possible to visit during Saturday afternoons when they are being cleaned in preparation for Sunday.

In July and August in particular it is extremely hot in Spain during the day, with temperatures well up into the nineties (or even higher in Navarre) and very little shade at all, apart from many areas of Galicia. The best way to avoid walking in the heat is to get up before it is light and set out at daybreak (though not before or you won't be able to see the way). At this time of day it is cool and pleasant, with the added advantage of being able to watch the sun rise as you walk and enjoy the scenery in the early morning light. In this way, even with stops, you should be able to reach your destination by 1 or 2pm, when you can eat and rest awhile before going out sightseeing/visiting in the (relative) cool of the early evening. It is also a good idea, in large towns and other places of any size, to go for a *paseo* in the evening and check how you will leave, so as not to waste time or get lost the following morning.

c) Other practical information

Shops (eg. food) are usually open between 9 or 10am and 2pm and then again between 5 and 8pm. In small villages you may have to ask where these are (though in such places bars often double up as shops as well) and be prepared for them not to be well stocked with what you need: in remote places the lines carried are often only very basic and limited in range.

Meals. These are much later than in Britain: 1.30 to 3.30 for lunch and 8.30 or 9pm until 11pm for evening dinner. However, as most bars also provide tapas (different kinds of snacks) as well as (in many) bocadillos (sandwiches) you need not go hungry if you are feeling ravenous outside regular mealtimes. Breakfast, in hotels, fondas, etc., is rarely available before 9am.

Cafés and bars close very late but do not normally open before 8.30 or 9am and in small villages do not always serve hot drinks all day long. Remember that a "cafetería" is not a self-service restaurant but a bar that also serves things to eat for breakfast (such as cake or sandwiches).

Banks open from 8.30 till 2pm. Post Offices (Correos) are often open in the mornings only but stamps can also be bought in estancos (tobacconists).

Stamps for pilgrim passports. Modern pilgrims who seek proof of their pilgrimage also carry pilgrim "passports" which they have stamped at regular intervals along the Way (churches, town halls, etc.) and which they then present to the Cathedral authorities in Santiago to help them obtain their "Compostela" or certificate.

More information about this is available from the Confraternity of Saint James.

<u>Phones</u>. Phone boxes usually take coins though in large towns you will also find ones taking phonecards.

<u>Dogs</u>, their owners nearly always tell you, "won't hurt you", though this is often hard to believe. They may tell you, too, that it is the rucksack that bothers them (and as dogs are reputed to see only in black and white there may be some truth in this, faced with mysterious hump-backed monsters on two legs...), but it is not much comfort when faced with an aggressive one. They live all along the <u>camino</u>, tied up or, frequently, running around loose, hear you ages before you have any idea where they are and are often enormous (though the small ones are, in fact, a greater nuisance, as they have a nasty habit of letting you pass quietly by and then attacking from behind, nipping you in the back of your ankles). A <u>stick</u> is very useful, even though you might not normally want to walk with one - not to hit them with but to threaten. Be warned!

USING THIS GUIDE

a) Waymarking (see p6)

The route is described from the Spanish monastery at Roncesvalles to Santiago de Compostela, ie. in the direction of the (modern) pilgrimage. It is therefore described in one direction only, although for the benefit of those who would like to walk the Way in reverse or return on foot some hints have been included in the text [in square brackets] since the waymarking is also "one-way only" and often difficult to follow backwards, even if you have already walked the outward journey.

It is for this reason that, from time to time, the text contains such seemingly irrelevant remarks as "track joins from back L", redundant for those walking only towards Santiago but helpful for the person going in reverse and faced with a choice of paths to select.

Waymarking (<u>señalización</u>) is in the form of yellow arrows (<u>flechas</u>) or flashes (<u>señales</u>) painted on tree trunks, walls, road signs, rocks, the ground, sides of buildings etc., and are normally extremely easy to spot. They appear at frequent intervals and the walker will not usually encounter any difficulty following them, except, at times, in some areas where road construction is in progress. (If, at any time, they seem to have disappeared, this will be because you have inadvertently taken a wrong turning: retrace your steps to the last one you saw and start again from there, checking carefully.) Some sections are also waymarked with blue and white metal signs with the picture of a pilgrim in a hat while the beginning part of the walk, as far as Viana, has the red and white balises of the French GR system as well, as a continuation of the route through France from Le Puy. In Galicia, in addition, there are standardised concrete marker stones, about the size of old-fashioned milestones, bearing an embossed conch-shell design, the number of kilometres remaining to Santiago and the name of the village, hamlet or spot where they are located. They are positioned at 500m intervals and are not only attractive, providing reassurance that you are, in fact, on the right track (as indicated above, Galicia is criss-crossed with literally hundreds of old green lanes, involving constant changes of direction in some places), but they are also a useful way of knowing exactly where you are in villages that are too small to bear the usual placename signs. It is apparently planned, eventually, to extend this type of señal to the rest of the camino.

b) Maps

These are a problem. It is possible to follow the camino just with the waymarks and this guide but that would be very limiting. Maps are useful not merely as a means of finding the way when lost but also for situating the walk in the context of its surroundings and for any diversions you might wish to make to visit places of interest within striking distance of the route. At present there are no comprehensive, reliable Spanish equivalents of the Ordnance Survey maps of Britain or the French IGN series. In 1989, however, the Spanish IGN (Instituto Nacional Geográfico), in conjunction with MOPU (Ministerio de Obras Públicas y Urbanismo) published a map entitled _El Camino de Santiago_, covering the whole of the route on a scale of 1:600.000. This is not detailed enough to walk from but places the camino in the context of its surroundings and is readily available (from Stanford's map shop in London, or from the Map Shop, Upton-upon-Severn, for example). Otherwise two maps in the Michelin 1:400.000 (1cm:4km) series are recommended: 441 North West Spain and 442 Northern Spain.

c) Textual description

Each section begins with the distance walked from the previous one, a description of the facilities available, a brief history, where applicable, and an indication of the places of interest to visit. (Walkers wishing to spend time in any of the larger towns should obtain information leaflets and a street plan from the Tourist Office there.) The figures after each place name heading indicate the height in metres where known and, in parentheses, the distance in kilometres from both Roncesvalles and Santiago.

Place names appear in the text in bold type. Other names that help in wayfinding, such as street names, the names of prominent buildings, rivers, etc., appear in italics. "River", however, rarely implies a wide, deep, fast-flowing stretch of navigable water: most, if not actually dried up, are no more than narrow trickles at the bottom of a wide river bed and may be non-existent at certain times of the year.

Abbreviations have been kept to a minimum. L indicates that you should turn/fork left, R that you should turn/fork R. (L) and (R) mean that something you pass is to your left or right. KSO = Keep Straight On. UMUR = unmade up road. // = parallel. Km = kilometre, KM = kilometre marker (found on the sides of all main roads; K is reserved for the marker stones in Galicia). N followed by a number (eg. N135) refers to the number of a main road, C to the number of a local road.

* * * * * * *

The Way of Saint James is not a map and compass walk and very little of the walking is strenuous, though there are a couple of stiff climbs (up to El Cebreiro, for example, and over the Pyrenees for those starting on the French side). Timings have not been given from place to place but 4km per hour, exclusive of stops, is often considered average, especially when carrying a heavy rucksack. However, a comfortable pace may often be more than this - a fit walker may well be able to maintain a speed of 5 to 6km or 3^{1}/$_{2}$ miles per hour.

The route is practicable, though not necessarily recommended, all through the year. In winter the weather may be dry over much

27

of the route but as a lot of it is quite high up (Burgos, for instance, is at 2000 feet, though the area around it is more or less flat) it gets very cold, with a biting wind. In spring it rains a lot, especially in Galicia (Santiago has the highest average rainfall in Spain) and in Navarre. If you are not restricted to a particular time of year May/ early June or the autumn are best - dry, but not as hot as in summer, and accommodation is also much less crowded. Traditionally, though, as many people as possible aimed to arrive in Santiago for the festivities on July 25th, Saint James' day, particularly in Holy Years. Many still do.

Ultreya!

Puenta la Reina. Pilgrim bridge over the River Arga, (photo: Simon Derry)

The Route

Roncesvalles 925m (0/709)

Shop with guidebooks etc., hotel-restaurant, monastery-run posada, youth hostel. Walker pilgrims may stay in the refuge in the old hospital building after obtaining their "credencial" or pilgrim passport from the vice-abbott.

Augustinian monastery and hospital founded early in the twelfth century. Set in the "valley of thorns" in the foothills of the Pyrenees it has a long tradition of looking after pilgrims (it fed 25,000 a year during the seventeenth century). Collegiate church, chapel of Santiago, fourteenth-century royal pantheon containing the thirteenth-century tombs of Sancho the Strong and his wife Doña Clemencia of Toulouse. Museum with religious paintings and sculpture, treasury.

If you don't arrive on foot from Saint Jean-Pied-de-Port but want to start walking from Roncesvalles you can take the bus from Pamplona bus station (6pm except Sundays) to Burguete and then walk the remaining 3km.

MAP 1

Leave Roncesvalles by the main entrance (KM47 on the N135), walk along LH side of road for 20m then cross over at information board. *(Fourteenth-century pilgrim cross on L on way out of the village.)* Continue along a path shaded by trees, more or less // to road to begin with. After 2km you will reach a fence: go through it and then turn L to follow a cart track diagonally to two large white buildings by road. Cross cattle grid and continue R along road for 500m to

3km Burguete 893m (3/706)
2 hostals, 2 bars, 2 restaurants, bank, pharmacy.
   Basque village with splendid eighteenth- to early nineteenth-century houses on either side of the main street.

KSO down main street past modern church of *San Nicolás de Bari* and public garden and turn R along the side of the bank building. Cross track and stream after 20m, continue past large farm (R) and then to L over stream. Track continues through fields. Take L fork ahead through gate, cross stream, then another, into semi-shaded woodland. Go through barbed-wire fence and turn L. Cross stream and go uphill into woods. Go through another gate and KSO. [Another track joins from back L.] At top, veer L to descend, through farm, to road opposite modern church of *San Bartolomé* and tower of the *Biblioteca Pública* into

3.5km Espinal 871m (6.5/702.5)
Shop, 2 bars, panadería, restaurant.
   Basque village founded in 1269; houses with armorial devices above doorways.

KSO along main street and then turn L at house called *Aunta Mendi*, along road through fields. KSO at junction but 200m further on leave track as it veers L uphill and take small FP R alongside fence along edge of fields with spruce plantation and enter woods. *(View to rear over foothills to TV mast at Monte Orzanzurieta and Col Lepoeder.)* Follow path uphill into the open, turn L at top, joining path coming from R. Climb over stile at top, turn R along cart track and then veer L along ridge, through fields, downhill, under trees and cross the road at

1.8km Alto de Mezquiriz (Puerta de Espinal) 922m (8.5/700.5)
A new trilingual stele invites the pilgrim, in French, Spanish and Basque, to pray to Notre-Dame de Roncevaux.

After crossing the road do <u>not</u> go straight on through the gate and up the track, even though it might seem the most obvious path to take, but turn L instead, before you reach the fence, following the waymarks. *Here, as in many sections of the <u>camino,</u> the path plays hide and seek with the road, often running more or less parallel to it but shortcutting its many hairpins.*

Go through a gate (L) and continue downhill through beech woods. Veer R at fork *(waymarks here may be plastic tape)*. At the next fork take the lower path *(although you are still high up, // to road)*. Path veers R away from road, downhill to ladder stile. Turn L along old road to reach bend in modern road but then turn R immediately up old green lane with trees banked up on either side. Tracks join the <u>camino</u> from R (3 times) but KSO downhill all the way to the road. Turn R along it, pass a small junction 20m later and after a bend the path drops down to R at crash barrier at old road. It emerges at the road again after 50m (ie. short cuts for hairpins), just before the village of

3.5km Viscarret (12/697)
Small village with shop, the end of the first stage of the Way of Saint James as outlined in the <u>Codex Calixtinus</u> *(It began in S Michel-le-Vieux, 3km south of Saint Jean-Pied-de-Port.)*

10m further on the path drops to the R, / / to the road, joining the main street 50m further on. Continue along this, cross over road and KSO through village *(fountain on R)*. Follow road through village, veer R and shortly before leaving turn L down old road (1km) / / to new road. Cross over and turn R into green lane. KSO until you reach the village of

1.5km Linzoan (13.5/695.5)
Church on hill to L is a good place for a rest, shady, with good views.

From here to the Alto de Erro the route climbs uphill and then along a wooded ridge. Follow road through village past frontón, veer L *(fountain)* and then turn R uphill under footbridge over road. Road becomes a track, follow it to top, cross over UMUR and KSO. Lane

The cloisters of San Zoilo at Carrion de los Condes

The Canal de Castilla at Fromista
The Casa de Botines in Leon

continues to climb and then leads into UMUR coming from R. KSO for 800m and then leave track to L. KSO to cross roads and then KSO again for 2km till you pass a stone with "Roldán" painted on it. *This is the spot where Roland eventually decided - too late - to blow his horn to summon help from Charlemagne and his army, as related in the Song of Roland. Shortly afterwards you will see Zubiri in the distance below, through a clearing in the trees, with its large magnesita factory.* 1km further on reach the road (C135) at

3.5km Alto de Erro (Puerta de Erro) 810m (17/692)

Cross the road *(the stone construction opposite covers a former well, much used by pilgrims)* and KSO through more woods. After 1km pass to the L of an old building: this is the *Venta del Caminante or Venta del Puerto, a former pilgrim inn.* Follow the track as it gradually loses height, watching out carefully for the waymarks. After 3km you will reach the old medieval bridge over the *Arga* at

4.2km Zubiri 526m (21/688)

Bar, restaurant (both may have rooms), shop, bank, panadería.

The name Zubiri means *"village with the bridge"* in Basque. The bridge itself was known as *"el puente de la rabia"* because, so the story goes, any animal that crossed it three times was cured of rabies. The large building immediately to the R before you cross the bridge was a former hospital, possibly a leprosarium.

If you want to go into the village cross the bridge *(fountain on other side, next to church).* If not, turn L along path just before it (waymarked), between two large houses, down green lane. Cross footbridge over stream and KSO. Take R fork downhill. The path follows the valley of the River *Arga.* Pass electricity sub-station (R) and join minor road opposite factory. Follow this for 300m then fork R to join track coming from factory, / / to road. KSO when you reach UMUR and fork L under electricity cables to valley bottom.

Be careful not to miss the next turning: cross footbridge over stream, enter green lane and KSO to hamlet of **Ilarraz** *(fountain on L).* Turn R down minor road, pass church (R) and continue to junction at bend in road. Turn L along this road to hamlet of **Esquirroz.** KSO at junction but then turn R at last house and continue straight on into a green lane (waymarked). KSO. Cross stream at footbridge. KSO, passing a large battery hen farm (L). Follow path along edge of field, join farm track from L and KSO to minor road. Turn L and then R 20m further on across a field, following marker posts (tall hedge to your R). Cross two more fields, continue along short green lane, through one more field, enter another green lane and follow it to junction with minor road at house (R) at entry to village of

5km Larrasoaña (26/683)
Fountain (no shop).

Village founded as a monastery, later donated to Leyre, formerly with pilgrim hospitals. Church contains statue of Saint James.

To go into Larrasoaña: turn R, cross bridge and then turn L at church. To continue: turn L onto road and follow it to hamlet of **Aquerreta** *(fountain)*. Turn R down a track and after a few yards continue straight on, down a green lane that might not seem obvious at first. KSO. Pass through a spruce plantation and cross another field. Enter woods and KSO. Go through clédo and KSO. Follow path down to river and bear L along the bank, taking upper (LH) track when it divides. KSO along river for 2km, passing weir in river (R) shortly before reaching modern bridge over the River *Arga* at

3.5km Zuriain (29.5/679.5)
Cross bridge and veer L onto main road at end of village. Continue along main road for 50m and then turn L down minor road signposted "Ilurdoz 3". Cross bridge over the *Arga* back on to the LH bank again and take R turn at bend in road almost immediately afterwards, past some modern houses. Pass between remnants of a fort above you on the hill (L) and then, maintaining your height, continue straight on below the terrace of a very large house (L). *At this point the path is halfway up a hill, // to the river and to the main road beyond.*

KSO then turn L round the side of a large white house, cross bridge, pass *fountain* (L) and fork R at church. Continue on UMUR, following it round bend to R and cross restored medieval bridge over the *Arga* to the village of **Uroz**. *If you have not already come across this phenomenon before - in the south of France, for example - you will encounter here the first of many church clocks that strike twice for every hour (and therefore 24 times at midnight...). Since they do not have the "ding dong ding dong" prelude to the actual hour strokes that are* *customary on British public clocks the first series is, in effect, an announcement that the hour is going to strike - for the second time - after a couple of minutes' pause.* Turn L along main road for 600m to

2.8km Zabaldica (32.5/676.5)
Church contains statue of Saint James but is usually kept locked so to see it you will have to ask for the key at a nearby house.

Turn R up steep hill below church and then turn L after 15m on to a path // to road below. Watch out carefully for the waymarks here and follow the path as it drops down to the road at the old road bridge, now a layby. Take RH path uphill and follow the path as it takes you high up, // to road below and to the river again, with the water towers of the Pamplona water authority in a line above you. *(From here you can see the village of Huarte in the distance to your L and the Romanesque Ermita de la Virgen de la Nieve over on the hill on the opposite side of the river.)* Follow the waymarks which lead you through fields for 1km until you reach the main road. Either cross it carefully) at road level or use the tunnel under it (a concrete tube) and turn R along the service road. This then veers L and leads, after a few hundred yards, to the bridge over the river *Ulzama (a tributary of the Arga)* at

3.5km Trinidad de Arre (36/673)
Immediately after the bridge, on the R, is the Basilica de la Sanctissima Trinidad, where there was also a small pilgrim hospital in former times. Turn L after crossing the bridge (fountain on R) and enter

0.6km Villava (37/672)
Suburb of Pamplona.

Go along main street for 1km past public garden (L) and bear (R) to cross roads with traffic lights. Continue straight ahead along a tree-lined paseo *(note elaborate Basque style school of agriculture on R)* and enter suburb of

1km Burlada (38/671)
Shops etc.

When you reach some traffic lights with a Renault dealer (R) and the *Villa Josepha* with a large, tree-filled garden (L) <u>do not</u> continue straight ahead to cross the river by the road bridge but cross the road and turn R along the *Calle Larraizar* with a school on its R, past a block of flats, to the main road. Cross this carefully and KSO on other side along a minor, tree-lined road, the *Camino* or *Carretera Burlada*, for 2km.

At a bend in the road you will get a good view of Pamplona cathedral and then note (L) two houses with their façades decorated all over with scallop shells embedded in the stucco. When you have almost reached the river *(fountain on R by school)* a minor road crosses the one you are on. Turn R and then almost immediately L over the *Puente de los Peregrinos, the old pilgrim bridge over the River Arga with a recently decapitated statue of Saint James on a small column at the far end.* Cross the public garden straight ahead towards the town walls, following waymarks, cross road at traffic lights diagonally R and KSO to walk between the inner and outer sets of ramparts. At the gateway KSO up the *Calle del Carmen* into the old quarter of

2km Pamplona 415m (40/669)

Population 200,000. All facilities. RENFE, buses to Burguete, Puenta la Reina, Estella, Logroño. Map shop opposite the cathedral.

*The end of the second stage of the Camino de Santiago in Aymery Picaud's guide. A fortress town situated on rising ground in the middle of a broad valley Pamplona (Iruna in Basque) was the capital of the ancient kingdom of Navarre and is the capital of the modern autonomous **región** of the same name. It is probably most famous today for the festival of San Firmin during the first two weeks of July with the "running of the bulls", but it also contains many places of interest (the Tourist Office, Calle Anumada, near the Plaza de Castillo, produces a useful leaflet for a walking tour of the city) and it is worth spending at least half a day here. Gothic cathedral with outstanding cloisters, churches of San Sernin, San Domingo, San Nicolás and San Lorenzo. Museo de Navarra, Ciudadela (fortress area, now a park).*

To visit the cathedral: turn off the *Calle del Carmen* at a small square with a statue. To continue: KSO along the *Calle del Carmen* and then turn R into the *Calle de Mercadores. (The route through Pamplona is well-waymarked with the blue and yellow Council of Europe arrow signs.)* Veer R into the *Calle San Saturnino*, past the church of *San Sernin* (L), after which turn L into the *Calle Mayor.* KSO along

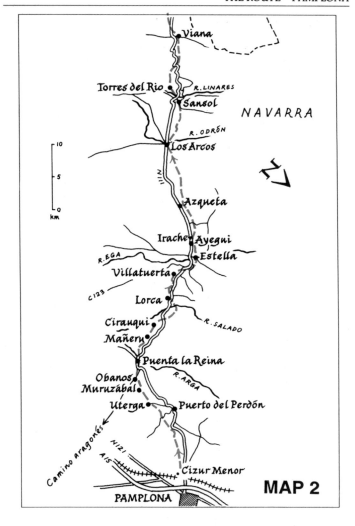

MAP 2

this, past the church of *San Lorenzo* (L), cross over the road and KSO ahead along the *Calle del Bosquedillo*. Veer L to parkland surrounding the *Cuidadela* and follow the flagstone path (waymarked). When it turns in front of the *Cuidadela* veer R across the grass to the road. Cross this and continue down the *Calle Fuente de Hierro*, which leads downhill across the *campus of the University of Navarre* and then becomes the *Camino de Santiago*.

Continue ahead along a minor road signposted to "Cizur Menor", crossing the bridge first over the River *Sadar* and then the River *Elorz*. KSO. When the modern road forks to the L, fork R, KSO and cross the railway track (carefully). Continue ahead and this path then becomes the pavement along the main road to the L, which it then joins. KSO to top of the hill to the village of

4km Cizur Menor 483m (44/665)
Bars, restaurant (but no shop), fountain in public garden (R).

Restored Romanesque church on R of main road, remains of the twelfth-century commandery of the Knights of Saint John of Jerusalem and the old pilgrim hospital on L. From here onwards there is very little shade. Continue on road and turn diagonally R 20m after public garden at frontón along a line of trees (now on L). Turn R at crossroads and KSO past houses into open country, along UMUR through fields. KSO as road bends R at last house. KSO at next T junction and continue uphill. [Road joins from R as you start going uphill.] KSO, veer L, KSO for 200m then turn R diagonally onto track and KSO. At four solitary trees do not turn L but KSO. *The village of* **Galar** *and the Monte del Perdón* **(1,037m)** *are visible ahead to the L.* When track ends at another group of trees KSO through field.

Follow path as far as bank, climb it (remains of steps), turn R then L after a few yards and KSO. *A piece of triangular masonry (a ruined house) is visible ahead. Church and hamlet of* **Guendulain** *above you to the R.* KSO, cross track, KSO slightly uphill all the time. *Good view back to Pamplona if it is is not too hazy.* KSO to village of

4km Zariegui 570m (48/661)
Cross road *(Romanesque church on R)* and KSO for 1km, downhill at first and then up again. Fork R on to a smaller path at sign marked "A Santiago" on open hillside and continue wending your way

uphill.

Shortly before passing under the electricity cables there is a splendid modern fountain (though not necessarily working) on your L at a spot named **Gambellacos**. *Legend has it that a pilgrim making his way up to the Alto del Perdón, exhausted and overcome by a terrible thirst was accosted by the devil, disguised as a walker, who offered to show him a hidden fountain but only on condition that he renounce God, the Virgin Mary or Saint James. The pilgrim refused but then Saint James himself, disguised as a pilgrim, led him to the hidden fountain and gave him water to drink in his scallop shell.*

Reach the road after 100m at

5km Alto del Perdón 780m (53/656)

Panoramic views ahead to Puente la Reina and laid out in front of you, like a map, are the villages you will pass through next: **Uterga, Muruzábal** *and* **Obanos**.

Cross over the road and go down the other side, veering R. Go through fence and onto open heathland, watching out carefully for the waymarks. Join a wide stony track and after 1km fork L (you can see a windmill at the bottom of the R fork). Continue downhill, veer L and KSO to gate.

KSO, turn R at fork and KSO. Track evens out, becoming less steep and winds through fields. [1km from gate track is joined by one coming from R.] KSO. Cross small river (with a long line of trees along its bank) and go uphill again into village of

3km Uterga (56/653)

KSO through village (*fountain*) and continue along quiet road to

3km Muruzábal (59/650)

Bar, fountain.

Go through village and as you are leaving it turn R diagonally, just before a large roadside cross (R). Go down FP for a few yards and turn L, walking along the edges of several fields. Then KSO up hill past rubbish tip (R) and fork R at top of hill into village of

2km Obanos 414m (61/648)

Bank, restaurant, panadería.

Ermita San Salvador, where the route from Roncesvalles is joined by the one coming from Arles over the Somport pass. A short detour is recommended from here to the twelfth-century church at Eunate, 3kms away on the Monreal/Las Campanas road. It is an octagonal building surrounded by a series of arches and was used as a burial place for pilgrims.

Enter the village by the *Camino Roncesvalles*. KSO to *Calle San Juan,* turn R into the *Calle Julia Gavarge,* L down a tree-lined street with a school (L) to church (public garden on its R). Continue diagonally through archway and KSO, following road as it bends to R past the *Ermita San Salvador* (L). When the road becomes a rough track at the side of a farm (R) KSO above vines (to L) and follow it down to the main road.

Turn L along it. Ignore yellow arrow to L after 100m opposite a large warehouse and KSO on road for a further 300m to junction with the N111. *Here there is a modern statue of a pilgrim to mark the junction of the caminos <u>francés</u> and <u>aragonés</u>.* Turn L along the N111 for 300m to

2km Puenta la Reina 346m (63/646)

Population 2000. All facilities. Buses to Estella, Logroño and Pampelona.

The town gets its name from the eleventh-century pilgrim bridge over the River Arga. This was built at the command of Queen Urraca, daughter of Alfonso VI and with its six arches remains unchanged today. It is also one of the most interesting on the <u>camino</u>. Church of Santiago (with statue of Saint James the pilgrim inside).

Turn L at refugio, a 2 storey building on the corner, with an arcaded verandah outside, and then turn R in front of the seminary, passing between it and the church of *Santiago* (R). KSO down the *Calle Mayor* until you get to the old bridge over the *Arga.* Cross it and turn L on to road. Cross main road (near modern bridge) and fork L onto minor road, // to main road. When this veers R, back towards the main road, at large wayside cross, fork L onto UMUR, which then becomes a cart track, running // to the river. Continue along it for 2kms and then, when you see a modern (water or electricity) tower across on the other side of the river to your L you will see a turning off to your R onto a wide track. Take it, go uphill and then turn L into a small valley.

You will see the main road high above you, which is where you are aiming for. Watch out carefully for the waymarks, bending R, follow track (by now a very small FP) and then bend L and KSO up an embankment into a newly cut-out UMUR which has had trees planted along it. Turn R along this and follow it to the main road, which it joins after climbing a steep embankment. Turn L. After approx. 200m the path follows the road but on the inside of the crash barrier. At the end of the barrier bear L and then L again down a minor road to the village of

4.5km Yesos Pamplona (67.5/641.5)
Follow road, veering L, cross bridge at R. KSO along *Calle de la Esperanza,* cross square diagonally and leave by LH top corner. Turn R and leave village along *Calle Forforza, Camino de Santiago.*

KSO, passing cemetery (L), grove of trees (L) and then fields. *(View of Ermita de Aniz on the hillside above you to the R.)* The path then turns sharp L along a lane and immediately R along a lane with a wall along the RH side. KSO along edge of fields in a straight line, watching out for the waymarks. Cross track coming at right angles and KSO as track becomes a grassy green lane. KSO to village of

2.5km Cirauqui 498m (70/639)
Shop, bar, fountain in public garden. (Bar 100m to R on main road.)

Ancient hilltop village with Gothic church of San Roman. The route through Ciraqui is a bit complicated with all the turns indicated by the yellow arrows but, basically, you go round the bottom of the village in a clockwise direction and then continue the straight line you started on entering.

Turn L then R, go up hilly street between tall houses, cross another road, go through arch up hill and turn L into the square. Go down street on LH side of bar, turn R downhill, then R again round base of village. KSO to old paved Roman road which leads you over the river on the old bridge and continue till you reach the main road again, at a roundabout/turning area. Cross the road, go up a lane a few yards and then turn L onto a track. Follow this, keeping straight on L at any junctions (coming from the R). KSO. Cross bridge. KSO (L) at junction. KSO to top of hill, turn L at next junction. Path descends. KSO when you see the road ahead of you, turn R down a slope behind a hump at side of road. Go down, follow path in valley, cross over to other side of stream and when you reach a track, cross it and continue in front of small white house. KSO. [Path joins track from R.] KSO. Shortly afterwards path joins another from R. Continue down to road and follow wall to road junction (150m). Here you will see signs for "Embalse de Alloz" (a reservoir).

Continue R along path (signpost says "Camino de Santiago"). Follow road under modern aqueduct and after houses on L turn L through 2 green gates onto a path which goes over an old bridge. This crosses the River *Salado (Salt River), one of the many rivers that Aymery Picaud warned pilgrims neither to drink themselves nor allow their horses to do so or they would die immediately. He also relates how he saw two Navarrese sitting there, sharpening their knives in preparation for flaying any pilgrim's horses who had the misfortune (as did his own) to drink there.*

Follow the path from the bridge and it will lead you under the modern road. On the other side turn R up an old road and follow it to village of

5km Lorca 483m (75/634)
Bar (has rooms), fountain.

Go through village (bar R) and down street to main road. KSO past another junction with electricity transformer to cross roads (minor roads) at top of hill. Turn L off road and then R after 20m to track between fields. 20m later turn R again onto a grassy track. KSO *(Village of Villatuerta visible ahead.)* After 1km approx. track reaches UMUR coming from L; continue along it.

Ignore the <u>old</u> waymarks indicating a L turn by six solitary tall trees but KSO till you reach the road. Turn L and continue to junction and turn L again into village of

2km Villatuerta (77/632)
KSO through village to old bridge. Cross it and continue L uphill to church *(good place for a rest, good view)* and KSO (church to your L). On leaving village cross a minor road. KSO along lane flanked by fields higher on R than on L. KSO until you reach main road. Cross it and veer L along grassy track (grove of trees on L, field on R). At end of 1st field KSO down lane and take L turn at fork, going steeply down to road. Turn R and continue along the road to Estella (2kms).

This section of the path plays hide and seek with the main road a lot and therefore sounds a lot more complicated than it actually is.

The outskirts of Estella are not very prepossessing: cemetery on R up hill, factories on L. Bar on L at entrance to town.

After 1.5km a L turn is indicated (yellow arrow) just after passing a funeral hardware merchant on R. This takes you along a lane behind the houses on the main road and // to it as far as a L bend in the road near the River **Ega**.

6km Estella 426m (83/626)

Population 13,000. All facilities. Hotels, buses to Pampelona, Puenta La Reina, Logroño. Tourist Office: Calle San Nicolás 3.

Estella (Lizarra in Basque) is the end of the third stage of the <u>camino</u> in Aymery Picaud's guide and contains several interesting Romanesque churches: San Pedro de la Rua, with very fine cloisters, San Miguel (now restored), San Juan Bautista, Santa María Jus del Castillo, San Sepulcro. The Palacio de los Reyes de Navarra is a rare example of a secular Romanesque building, with some well-known capitals, including Roland and the Moorish giant Ferragut.

On entering the town do <u>not</u> follow "centre city" traffic signs over road bridge over river but fork R, past sign "Estella" in tiles on a building in front of you and then turn L over a (very) steep hump-backed bridge. Turn R on the other side to the *Plaza San Martín (fountain).*

To leave Estella carry straight on along *Calle San Nicolás* (ie. behind Palacio). KSO and pass under archway at end of street to a road junction (church on your L). KSO on this (main) road, which divides after 300m. Cross over to the RH side and take the R fork, up an UMUR next to a petrol station and go up hill. Bear R at a factory and KSO to village of

2km Ayegui (85/624)

Just <u>before</u> you reach a square (houses, flats) and the top turn L and then R *(Monastery of Irache visible ahead from here)* and go downhill to road. Cross it and turn L up a lane to the twelfth-century church and **Monastery of Irache** (500m), *one of the first Benedictine houses in Navarre. It had a pilgrim hospice attached which was famous all along the pilgrim route. Fountain and picnic area.*

KSO up lane. When you reach a residential area turn R down 1st street (ie. <u>behind</u> the 1st line of houses you see) and follow this till you come to the main road (approx. 500m) opposite a hotel. Turn L along path parallel to road and continue along this for 4kms. The path joins the road just before the road enters a tunnel. Cross the road and enter the village (fountain on R) of

5km Azqueta (90/619)
Turn L at church, follow signs through village back to road. *(This is to avoid using the road tunnel.)* At "stop" sign turn R down a track to a farm. Go to the R of it (ie. building on your L) and turn L on to a path through fields and then alongside a wall. When wall starts to veer R go through a gap in it and follow the track on the other side through vines. Pass a restored building (R) that looks like a double-arched church doorway but is in fact a well and continue to village of

1km Villamayor (91/618)
Turn L onto road *(below church, Romanesque)* and then after 100m, opposite entrance to a lane, turn L down a FP that cuts through several bends in the "hairpins" in the road. Continue a short distance on this road and then turn R onto a UMUR and continue for 2km. Cross a road and KSO.

The walking in the quiet, gently undulating section between Villamayor and Los Arcos is easy (though watch out for the waymarks) and very pleasant in either very early morning or late evening light. There are no villages, no roads and almost no buildings at all along the way, woods over to the L and, later, large rock shapes ahead to the R.

About 1km after you have passed a modern barn and two ruined buildings turn R below another ruin on a hill. *(This is a short cut, joining the same track again after 100m but avoiding quite a lengthy "meander".)* Turn R onto UMUR again. Watch out for a turning to the L later on, well waymarked (arrows on RH side of track) but difficult to see where the path goes to. If you have trouble here, KSO for another 50m, turn L at junction and you will rejoin the waymarked path again about 1km further on your L.

KSO along this track, which leads you eventually to Los Arcos ahead in the distance, shortly before which it curves round to the R after a stone "seat" with waymarks on it.

10km Los Arcos 447m (101/608)
Population 1500. 2 hostals (one with bar), shop, bank, pharmacy. Buses to Estella, Pamplona and Logroño.

Small town with an arcaded square. Church of Santa María with Gothic cloister and interesting choir stalls in flamboyant Gothic interior. Several houses with armorial devices on façades in the long Calle Mayor.

Enter the town from the north past farm buildings. Turn L at fork and go down the full length of the *Calle Mayor* till you reach a small triangular "square" at the bottom. Turn R to church *(fountain)*. KSO (church on L) through archway ahead, cross road and then bridge over River *Odrón*, past public library (R). KSO taking R fork uphill past cemetery (R), *Capilla de San Blas* (L), electricity substation (L) into open countryside. *From here you will be going more or less // to the road and on a clear, non-hazy day you will have a good view of Sansol 6km away in the distance. There is very little shade at all in this section but the walking is easy, through fields and vineyards, and is well waymarked.*

Ignore turn to L, KSO and then turn R (just after the track goes into a dip) alongside a banked-up field. Carry on along the bank between two fields and when you meet another track crossing diagonally KSO (ie. R fork). KSO along this track, gently downhill into fields. After approx. 1km it is joined by another coming from the R. KSO. Cross a bridge over stream and KSO. When you reach a minor road turn L and follow it into village of

6km Sansol 505m (107/602)
Small hilltop village with very few modern buildings. Food shop inside another one marked "tabac" in main square.

This village gets its name from San Zoilo (the patron saint of its church, worth a visit, if it is open, for its frescoes of the Ascension and Gothic statue of San Pedro). Very good aerial view of Torres del Río from the forecourt in front of the church (and from where you can also see the path you will take to reach it).

At entry to village turn R into *Calle Mayor*, L into *Calle Real*, R into next street (uphill), next L, next R, next L and you will come out on the road again. Cross it and just opposite a notice board for Torres del Río *(below you now, on a hill top across the River Linares)*, climb over

the crash barrier and go down a small FP on the road's embankment
to a minor road 20m below. Turn L and then R down a small FP
leading to a bridge (dogs!). Cross it *(fountain/lavedero on L)*. Turn R
towards a large stone cross on top of a wall, L uphill into village of

1km Torres del Río (108/601)

*Another small village with very few modern buildings. Twelfth-century
octagonal Romanesque church of Santo Sepulcro showing influence of
Byzantine and Hispano-Arabic style (ask for key to visit). Fountain near
second church.*

To continue, fork L at church. Follow road to L then R uphill out
of village through orchards, past cemetery (L) to open fields. *This
section climbs up and down quite a lot, playing hide and seek to avoid the
very many hairpin bends in the main road and thus goes in a fairly straight
line, though constantly up and down.*

After 1km approx. descend to crossing with another track. KSO
(olive groves on R) and pass below the bend in one of the roads many
hairpins. Follow track down, then up, fork R to join road at a bend.
Turn L along road for 300/400m and you can then either:
a)   follow yellow arrows and stay on road;
b)   avoid a stretch on the road by turning R and then up along a
bank on its RH side, // to road. Pass through and then above a fir
plantation.

Both paths meet up again at the **Sanctuario de Nostra Señora
del Poyo** on RH side of road. Shortly further on, *an Ermita (near
Bargota). Panoramic views from here.*

Continue along road for 200m until next bend (N111 Km 72),
cross to other side and at end of crash barrier, turn R off road up lane
and then L after 20m up small path, following its zigzags to the top
of the hill. *(You can see Sansol behind you, three trees on hill to R.)* Go
along lane past building (L) and join road again after 200m. Turn L
and after 20m turn R along UMUR, taking R fork (it divides almost
immediately). *From here you can see both Viana and Logroño away in the
distance below you.*

Continue along path, KSO at next fork and follow path as it
zigzags down to valley floor, watching out for the waymarks
(balises, flechas and yellow tape) as you go, in a general diagonal
direction towards Viana. At the bottom, cross through an olive

grove, go up the slope on the other side, turn L onto a track coming from the R. Continue downhill (track joins from R after approx. 200m). Fork L at bottom, then R after 100m near small white house. 200m; later turn L along track coming from the R. (You can see the road over to your L, more or less // here.) When you reach a wood, bear L diagonally uphill (wood on your R). KSO at top past farm building (L) to road. Cross it and turn L into grassy lane. *(Here you are aiming for a future bend in the road near the electric pylons/cables at the top of the hill.)* Follow path straight up hill (watching out for waymarks) and join road again near (but not going under) cables. Turn L along road. After 200m turn L off road (ie. road bends to R but you continue more or less in a straight line) along grassy track. KSO. Cross another track and KSO till you rejoin road. Continue on road for 1.5km into

10km Viana (118/591)
Population 3,500. All facilities.

Attractive small town with cobbled streets and a long association with pilgrims (there were formerly four hospitals). Church of Santa María (almost as grand as a cathedral), fifteenth/sixteenth century, mixture of styles, with the tomb of Cesar Borgia under the street in front of it. Numerous houses with armorial devices on their façades. The Parque San Pedro (behind remains of church of that name) on part of the old town walls is a good place for a rest, with excellent views.

Leave Viana from the Plaza in front of the church by the *Calle Navarro Villoslado*. Turn R in front of the ruined church of *San Pedro (façade interesting)*, R diagonally then L *(Calle San Felices)* under arch. R again (same street name) to the road. Cross it and take the 2nd turn L (down street behind some seats) and zigzag R to *Calle El Rancho*. At the bottom cross the road and turn R by a large school, along a track which veers L past the school's sports ground. Continue alongside a long brick wall (R) and R again ie. going around the boundary of a small holding. Cross stream when you reach it and continue L along lane (100m) to a road. Cross it and KSO under electric cables to farm (R). Turn L at side of dog-kennel (*occupied!*) with waymark on it and veer R downhill under embankment to lane coming from L. Take 2nd fork R and KSO (L at next fork) until you get to another road. Cross it, turn L after 50m into a UMUR

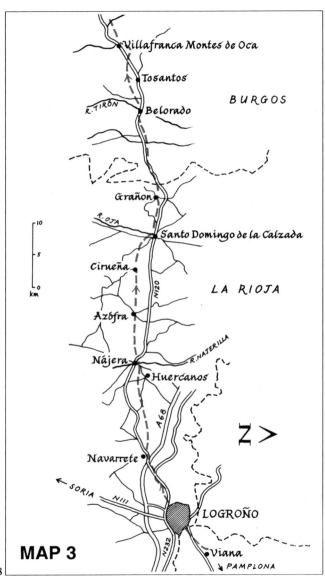

Villafranca Montes de Oca

Tosantos

R. TIRÓN

Belorado

BURGOS

Grañon

R. OJA

Santo Domingo de la Calzada

Cirueña

LA RIOJA

N120

Azofra

Nájera

R. NAJERILLA

Huercanos

A68

N >

Navarrete

← SORIA   N111

LOGROÑO

N232

Viana

↓ PAMPLONA

MAP 3

48

Camino entering Logroño

signposted "Virgen de Cuevas". *From here Logroño is visible ahead.*

Fork R (there are 2 turns to L) on UMUR through fields until you get to **Virgen de Cuevas** (1km), *once a chapel, now a private house, by a stream, a shaded area with a lot of trees and picnic area (fountain). Good view back over to Viana.*

20m later UMUR forks into three - take centre path and then fork R 100m later past farm. After 1km you will see a wood ahead of you near the road: watch out carefully for the waymarks as the route has recently been changed here and takes you to the road, which you then cross and continue on a FP through a small wood on the other side, // to the road. The path eventually takes you back to the road, near a paper packaging factory; cross bridge over a stream (petrol station on L) and enter the province of La Rioja.

Walk along hard shoulder and then on the footpath on RH side of road marked "Logroño norte" and at N111 K337 (post) cross to LH side of road. Turn left off it after 10m onto UMUR. *(This is indicated by the first of the many special "Camino" signs you will see, metal notice boards depicting a pilgrim with staff and hat in "pinman" format.) Shortly further on (10m) you will also see the first of another type of marker - a concrete stele, a little larger than a traditional milestone, with a scallop shell embossed on it. The red and white balises of the French GR system, used simultaneously with the yellow arrows, stop at Logroño for the moment).*

KSO along this UMUR, slightly uphill for most of the way, across a road, through fields and vines. The town of *Oyon* is visible away to the R on the other side of the road.

After 2km the UMUR descends downhill into Logroño, past a warehouse (R) and a few small houses to L and R. At the bottom you reach the main road into the town alongside the River *Ebro*, passing the cemetery to your R. Turn R along this road, then cross the stone bridge L over the river into

8km Logroño (126/583)

Population 120,000. Large bustling city with all facilities. RENFE. Buses to Pampelona, Burgos, Madrid. Tourist Office: Calle Miguel Villanueva 10.

Cathedral of Santa María Redonda, with a carving of Saint James in the choir stalls. Churches of Santiago, San Bartolomé (interesting portal) and Santa María de Palacio. Logroño is a large town today but it owes its development to the pilgrim route and the old quarter of the town is laid out along the line of the camino.

On the other side of the bridge take the second turn R down the *Calle de la Rua Vieja*, through the old quarter of the town, as its name suggests. At the end, continue along the *Calle de Barriocepa* to the *Fuente de los Peregrinos* in the *Plaza Santiago (with its modern checkerboard paving depicting sites along the route to Santiago on both the caminos aragonés and francés)* and then to the church of Santiago with its massive equestrian statue of Santiago Matamoros, Saint James the slayer of Moors, above the south door. (*This is best viewed from a distance, down the Calle de Santiago opposite.*)

Continue along the *Calle de Barriocepa* to the end, where it bends round to the L, turn R, R again and then L under an arch in the old town walls. On the other side turn L and then immediately R (*Calle de los Depositos*) past a roundabout with *fountains (and tap)* to your L (*well waymarked*). Cross a road L and then turn R down *Calle del Marques de Murieta*. Continue down this road for some time, past the barracks of the Guardia Civil and a large complex of older buildings called "Hogar Provincial". After crossing the railway line the road changes its name to *Avenida de Burgos*.

About 500m after this fork L behind a petrol station into an industrial estate. After the road veers L turn R between two factory buildings, one on either side of the road. KSO to a less minor road, cross it and KSO into open country (100m) after the road crosses an

irrigation channel. Continue for 300m until you get to a dual carriageway, cross it and turn R alongside it. When this road bends L to go to a factory turn R diagonally between the main road and the one leading to the factory, along a new gravel <u>camino</u> which has recently been planted with trees on either side. This is easy to follow and leads, after 2km, to the **Pantano de la Gragera** (a reservoir). When you get to a minor road (at a bend in it) fork L and then R along the wall of the dam. Cross a bridge at the end and veer L to woods *(bar/ restaurant to R)*.

The path leads round the side of the reservoir and then turns R at the end on to a track. After 20m, at a crossing with another track do not keep

Logroño. Church of Santiago el Real with equestrian statue of Santiago Matamoros

51

straight on (the old route) but turn L onto this track. KSO, ignoring turn to L and after 500m or so emerge onto the main road at the top of the hill. Continue on the hard shoulder of the N232 (*good view of Logroño behind you*). After 1km take L fork (N120) towards Navarrete. After 200m cross this road and fork R down a UMUR through vines, fields and over the motorway. To the L are the ruins of the old *Hospital of the Order of San Juan de Acre, founded in 1185 to look after pilgrims.* Follow the track down to a farm immediately below another road. [RJ: head for the silhouette of an <u>enormous</u> bull on the skyline.] Turn L diagonally up some steps to this road, cross it and follow the street into the village of

10km Navarrete (136/573)
Population 1500. Shops, bars, restaurant, bank. Several fountains. Campsite, fonda.

Navarrete has two "Calles Mayor", <u>alta</u> and <u>baja</u> (*both under restoration), arcaded and lined with <u>casas basonadas</u>, houses with heraldic devices on their façades. The town also has several <u>alfarerías</u>, pottery factories and workshops producing goods in the dark red clay seen everywhere in the landscape in this region. Monumental sixteenth-century church with a magnificent seventeenth-century Baroque reredos, gilded from floor to ceiling and wall to wall.*

To visit Navarrete: turn R up street in front of church and then either: a) follow yellow arrows along first street on L *(Calle Cal Neuve, roofed-in tunnel effect in first part)*; b) follow yellow arrows along second street on L *(Calle Mayor Alta)*. For a) turn R at end to join option b), at the end of which turn L at end of *Calle Mayor* to join *Calle de Santiago* (see below).

To continue towards Nájera: KSO past church (R) and public garden (L) then fork R up a slope *(Calle de Santiago)*. At the end of this road (it becomes the *Calle San Antonio* after some traffic lights) turn L down the *Calle Arrabal* and KSO when it is joined by a road coming from the L (it now becomes the *Calle San Roque*). Continue to a "stop" sign and then along the main road (ie. straight on).

KSO past the cemetery, *whose gates are the twelfth-century portals of the Hospital at the entrance to the village, installed there when the cemetery was established in 1875. Outside it there is a monument to a Belgian woman, Alice de Craemer, who was killed while riding a tandem to Santiago in 1986.*

Continue on the main road for 5km, watching carefully for the traffic. Just before the KM16 marker post there is a turning to the L, waymarked with a pinman pilgrim sign. Turn L along it then R down a lane that follows // to road. Cross a minor road leading from main road to Ventosa and KSO.

[To avoid the constant stream of juggernauts, cattle trucks, car transporters, ready-mix concrete lorries, huge vehicles laden with timber, clay, animals, etc, as well as cars and buses doing 100 kmph an alternative is available by turning L 1km approx. after passing the cemetery down a road marked "Sotés 3" and "Hornos 3". If you follow this to the village of Sotés and then on to Ventosa you can join the camino at the main road mentioned above, turning L. It is not waymarked but is easy to follow and although it is a couple of km longer is preferable to all the traffic on the busy main road.]

KSO through fields. 200m after hut (L) - *handy if raining* - track forks R, more steeply up hill, then forks R after 50m, up a grassy lane. Follow this uphill, then downhill, through vines, past a farm at **Alto de San Antón** *(and ruins of a convent with pilgrim hospital)*, when it meets the main road at a layby on a bend. (This is 2km after leaving the main road at KM16.)

Turn L, then R to cross road, go through gap in crash barrier, down steps in the embankment and turn L onto track at the bottom. Follow this for 3-4km, through fields, more or less // to the main road all the time. *Panoramic views.*

Ignore all turnings to L and after passing a stone hut (L) the track veers round to the R of a round hill (L). *This is the Poyo Roldán, where Roland is reputed to have slain the Syrian giant Ferragut with a huge stone, in the same way that David killed Goliath (from whom the giant is said to have been descended).* When you eventually reach the road at the cement/gravel works turn R and then L after 30m down a UMUR. Veer R past a mountain of sand/gravel and then cross a footbridge over the *Río Yalde (there is another memorial to Alice de Craemer here too).* Turn R after footbridge. Path veers slightly L. KSO along cart track between vines.

After 1km you reach a huge factory (with a pilgrim poem painted on its wall). Cross canal behind it (Canal Najerilla) and KSO 400m to minor road. Cross it and KSO along cart track until you come to a housing estate (blocks of flats). KSO into street *(bar and shop on R)* and continue into the centre of town, the road veering to the R as it nears the *Río Najerilla*.

16km Nájera (152/557)
Population 7000. All facilities.

End of the fourth stage of the camino in Aymery Picaud's guide. The town takes its name from the Arabic "place between rocks", a name which will become more obvious as you leave the town along a track which wends its way uphill between high cliffs on either side. Monastery of Santa María la Real, containing royal pantheon and interesting choir stalls with pilgrim scenes and cloisters. Church of San Miguel (Antigua), Convento de Santa Elena, Church of Santa Cruz. The present bridge (1886) over the River Najerilla replaces the twelfth-century bridge with seven arches built by San Juan de Ortega

On the other side of the river either follow the yellow arrows and turn R and then L, following the signs for the monastery or, a shorter, more direct way, turn L immediately after the bridge down the *Calle Mayor* (pedestrianised) to the end, into the *Plaza España* and turn R to the church of *Santa María* (set into cliff at rear).

Pass in front of the main entrance and KSO uphill. Continue on when road becomes a track, trees and woods to either side, uphill and then down (path is in a ravine here). Keep L at fork. KSO past farm (L), cross bridge and KSO ahead. At fork bear R. KSO. When track crosses another KSO along grassy track. When this eventually reaches a minor road [near tree, for RJ] turn L and continue along it for 1.5km to

6km Azofra 559m (158/551)
Village with 2 bars, shop, fountain in main square.

Church of Nuestra Señora de los Angeles with sculptures of Saint Martin of Tours and Santiago as a pilgrim, with staff, cape and hat. Just outside the village on the R is the Fuente de los Romeros, near the site of a twelfth-century pilgrim hospital with adjoining cemetery.

KSO down main street and continue to end of village. Turn R along main road for 50m then L along a farm road (UMUR). Ignore turns to L or R and KSO. After 1km pass a <u>rollo</u> (R), *a medieval pilgrim cross*. KSO. Turn R into UMUR and then L after 20m. Cross a minor road leading to *San Millán de Cogilla* and KSO, forking L after 10m. Turn L at next junction. KSO.

[The monasteries of San Millán de Cogilla - National Monuments - are definitely worth a visit but are situated 15km off the route to the south. The upper one, Suso, is Visigothic and contains the remains of San Millán, patron saint and protector of Castille. It dates from c.1000. The monumental lower monastery Yuso (it can only be visited on a guided tour) is mainly sixteenth to eighteenth century. Both are closed on Mondays. There is no accommodation at San Millán but there is a fonda 5km away at Badarán, on the way back to the camino.]

The original camino ran in a straight line from Nájera to Santo Domingo de la Calzada but today it is interrupted in three places by changes in land ownership and as a result there is a long stretch on the main road. However, the route described here is recommended, is waymarked, if somewhat sparsely, and is easy to follow. It is much quieter than the route using the "carretera" and has little traffic apart from the occasional tractor. It is a slightly longer route but has splendid views, taking you through undulating fields to the L of the village of Ciriñuela, passing by the edge of Cirueña.

When you come to another junction, in fact a diagonal crossroads, KSO. Continue for several km. After climbing, the route flattens out *(village of Ciriñeula plus church and cemetery over to R) and village of Cirueña visible ahead.* KSO till you come to it, turn R down road and then L after 300m on to a farm road between fields. Ignore any turns to L or R and continue for 3kms to

15km Santo Domingo de la Calzada (173/536)
Population 5000. All facilities.

The town takes its name from Santo Domingo (1019-1109), originally a shepherd, who wanted to enter the monastery of San Millán de Cogilla but was refused admission because he was illiterate. He then built himself a hermitage and chapel in a forest in a notoriously bandit-infested stretch of the camino between Logroño and Burgos and began to look after the needs of pilgrims. He built a hospital (today converted into a Parador) and church in what became the present-day town, a causeway and bridge over the River Oja and devoted the rest of his life to road and bridge building. One of his disciples, San Juan de Ortega, continued his work.

The town contains several places of interest (Convento de San Francisco,

Ermita de Nuestra Señora de la Plaza, Cistercian monastery, ramparts and tower) but the most well known is the Cathedral, where Santo Domingo is buried. However, what is most likely to strike the visitor are its two unusual occupants: a cock and a hen (both very much alive) in a cage high up inside the building, reminders of a miracle. A family of three pilgrims stayed in an inn in the town where the innkeeper's daughter is said to have made advances to the son, who refused the offer. In revenge she secretly placed a bag of money in his luggage and the following morning, after they had left, "discovered" that the money had gone missing. The innkeeper pursued the family, the son was brought before the judge and condemned to death. The parents continued their pilgrimage to Santiago, however, but on the return journey spent the night in Santo Domingo de la Calzada once again.

The mother was not convinced, in fact, that her son really was dead and went to the spot where he had been taken to be put to death and found him there alive, though still hanging. Accordingly the parents went to see the judge, to ask for their son to be released. Like his counterpart in the apocryphal account of the death of Judas Iscariot he too was sitting at dinner when the couple arrived and, likewise, refused to believe them. He declared that the boy was no more likely to be alive than were the cock and the hen on his table to get up and fly - which they immediately did, as proof of the son's innocence.

Enter town past farm/factory, continue along farm road when it bends to R to join road. Turn L to cross road (with <u>rollo</u>), cross over and take R fork past flats and then KSO down *Calle Mayor (fountain)*. Pass cathedral and KSO. Turn L at end of *Calle Mayor* and then R into *Calle de los Palmarejos* and KSO when it continues as *Avenida de la Rioja*. Cross the bridge over the *Río Oja (Ermita, 1917, at entrance to bridge)*.

After crossing the bridge and causeway walk along the main road for 6km. Turn off it L uphill between Km49 and Km50 and then immediately R uphill into the village of

6km Grañón (179/530)

Shop, bar, pharmacy.

Originally a walled town with two monasteries, a castle and a pilgrim hospital. Sixteenth-century Ermita de los Judios.

Cross road on entering village, go up short flight of steps and walk along main street past church (L). Continue a little further and then turn R (waymarked). At first it may seem as though you are going back on yourself but you then turn L by a modern barn building onto a minor road. Follow road round a bend after 200m (ie. do not go straight on) to barn with yellow arrow on it. Cross bridge over River *Relachigo* and take second L along farm road. Fork R after approx. 1km *(village of Recedilla del Camino visible ahead)* and follow track 1.5km to village. Just before you reach it turn R at farm to join road. Pass another rollo and *fountain* (R).

3km Recedilla del Camino (182/527)
Bar.

Between Grañon and Recedilla you pass from La Rioja into the province of Burgos. Village with a long tradition of looking after pilgrims (there were several hospitals here), its single main street lined with houses bearing armorial devices. Church of the Virgen de la Calle contains Romanesque font. Continue along main street at church *(fountain)* and public garden *(fountain)*. KSO to end of village and join road again (Km55 on leaving village). Continue on main road, cross bridge over River *Relachilo* (carefully - bridge is on a sharp bend).

2km Castildelgado (184/525)
Petrol station, bar/restaurant El Caserio (has rooms), Hostal Restaurant El Chocolatería. Church.

KSO along main road. Pass turning to *Viloria de la Rioja (2km to L, birthplace of Santo Domingo de la Calzada).*

4km Villamayor del Río (188/521)
Bar/restaurant. Fountain. (Despite its name this is not a "big town on a river" but only a "small village by a stream").

KSO on main road until just after K64. Turn R off road by warehouse, down lane leading, after 1km, to church of *Santa María* in

6km Belorado (194/515)
Small town with all facilities, population 2,000.

Churches of Santa María (sixteenth-century, contains a Santiago chapel) and San Pedro (seventeenth-century), used alternately, summer

and winter.

To leave - turn L (church on R), L again, R to arcaded main square. Cross it in a straight line (trees, bandstand) and go down the *Calle José Antonio de Ribera*. Turn L. Then either: turn L again, then R to main road or KSO behind blocks of flats, joining road at a sawmill. Turn R and KSO.

Cross the River *Tirón*, pass petrol station (L) after approx. 1km out of Belorado) and after 20m (<u>before</u> Km68) there is a turning to the L, down a minor road, signposted "San Miguel de Pedroso 3". Turn L here and then immediately R off it onto a track. Then, turn R again almost immediately and the lane you are now on is now //to main road and remains so, more or less, to Espinosa del Camino.

KSO, watching out carefully for waymarks. Cross a track and KSO along a grassy FP, joining a track from behind L and then another to side L. KSO and after 200m reach village of

3km Tosantos (197/512)
Bar 100m on main road. Cemetery uphill to L. Twelfth-century Ermita Virgen de la Peña set into hillside on the R, on other side of main road.

Do not go as far as the main road but fork L uphill up a farm road. Follow this to the village of

2km Villabistia (199/510)
Fork R just before passing church (R). KSO, cross bridge over river, pass *fountain* (R) and chapel of *San Roque* and KSO (ie. do <u>not</u> follow road round to R). *Village seems a bit run-down. Main road is still away to the R, more or less // to camino.*

KSO until you reach the road. Turn L and 20m later turn R into a lane and into village of

1.5km Espinosa del Camino (200.5/508.5)
KSO past *fountain* (R). Follow road round to R and then turn L behind the last line of houses onto a farm road. KSO, ignoring next three turns to R. After you pass the *Abside de San Felices (ruins of the medieval monastery of San Félix de Oca*, R) a UMUR leads round to the L *(view of Villafranca Montes de Oca ahead, with its large, prominent church).*

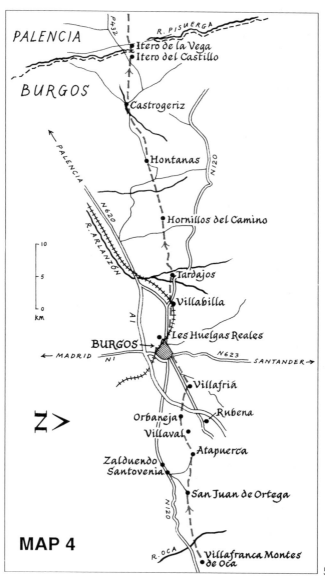

PALENCIA

R. PISUERGA

P432

● Itero de la Vega
● Itero del Castillo

BURGOS

● Castrogeriz

PALENCIA

● Hontanas

N120

N620

R. ARLANZÓN

● Hornillos del Camino

10

5

0

km

● Tardajos

● Villabilla

A1

● Les Huelgas Reales

BURGOS →

← MADRID   N1

N623

SANTANDER →

N >

● Villafría

Orbaneja ●

● Rubena

Villaval ●

● Atapuerca

Zalduendo ●
Santovenia ●

N120

● San Juan de Ortega

MAP 4

R. OCA

● Villafranca Montes de Oca

Continue till you reach the road. Turn R onto it and follow it to the village of

4.5km Villafranca Montes de Oca (205/504)

Bar/restaurant El Pajero has rooms. Shop, pharmacy, panadería, fountain.

"Town of the Franks", like others along the camino, the village's name refers to the many Frankish settlers and traders who established themselves along the pilgrim route in the Middle Ages. Situated at the foot of the Montes de Oca it had its own bishop until 1075 and an important pilgrim hospice as early as 884. This was superseded in 1380 by the thirty-six bed Hopital de San Antonio Abad, at present under restoration as a refuge. The eighteenth-century parish church of Santiago replaces an earlier building and contains a statue of Saint James.

Do not leave here late in the day and allow plenty of time. It is not difficult to find the way to San Juan de Ortega in good weather but it takes at least three hours and the route, at 1,150m, is wooded and completely unpopulated. In this section the waymarks are the Council of Europe blue and yellow signs with the Milky Way logo.

Go along main street and turn off to the R up the side of the church (L), pass remains of Hospital San Antonio (R) and continue uphill beside modern (long) wall. Pass trees and join farm road from L. Turn R along it *(level here and good views to rear on a clear day)*.

Fork R shortly afterwards to join another track coming from R (ie. a cross roads where, in fact, you KSO). KSO up hill and after 2km reach (signposted) the **Fuente de Mojapan** *(literally "moisten bread", a common pilgrim resting place in former times in an area too dangerous to cross at night and in which wolves were an expected hazard).*

After this the track enters the woods (semi-shaded) and veers to L. KSO, ignoring paths to L and R. Join forest road coming from L and KSO until you reach the memorial to those killed in the Civil War (R), the **Monumento de los Caidos** (alt. 1,163m). Descend steeply after this, cross the River *Peroja* and then climb up again. *(The path is in a dead straight line here, visible from the monument, // to main road and to main road being excavated between the two.)*

Path veers L and shortly after this (near road) fork R. After approx. 500m the path emerges into a very wide forest track. Turn R onto it at MP57 (post). [RJ: waymarks and MP57 hidden by trees. Flashes / yellow paint on pile of stones at R. Turn L to small unmarked

Camino in La Rioja

opening in embankment onto FP. This is approx. 100m after Council of Europe waymarking on R.]

At big crossing (MP61) and trig point type pillar KSO unless you want to visit the *Fuente del Carnero*, waymarked 200m to L. *(Signposted "fuente" in yellow.) This is at the side of the road, by the Ermita de Valdefuentes, all that remains of a former pilgrim hospital.*

After 1km join road coming from L [RJ fork L]. 1km further on a similar track joins from behind R. *A very large wooden cross has waymark on it.* KSO.

After a further 2km the church of *San Juan de Ortega (Saint John of the Nettles)* is visible for a while in the distance through the trees to the L. Turn L at next fork. After 500m track opens out, goes downhill and 500m further on you reach the church of

12km San Juan de Ortega 1,250m (217/492)
Small hamlet with the large pilgrim church of San Nicolás de Bari and monastery (recently restored), containing the elaborately decorated tomb of San Juan de Ortega. After his ordination the saint went on a pilgrimage to the Holy Land and on his return set up shelter for pilgrims in the notoriously dangerous and bandit-infested Montes de Oca. One of the most famous architects of his day San Juan de Ortega constructed the Romanesque church in such a way that at 5 o'clock in the evening on the spring and autumn equinoxes (21st March and 22nd September) - and only on those days - the rays of the setting sun light up the capital depicting the scene of the Annunciation. Instead of highlighting the angel Gabriel, as happens in most portrayals of this scene, it focuses instead on the Virgin Mary, thus transmitting the idea of fecundity and life. (The saint was also well known for his gift of making childless couples fertile.) Fountain.

Continue past the church till you reach the road. Cross it and enter woods. <u>Very</u> large wooden cross (some 15 - 20 feet high) and <u>cledo</u> shortly afterwards. KSO along forest road. Pass another large cross and another cledo. KSO. Road opens out, cross a ravine (path banked up across it). KSO and fork towards R at third large cross, descending towards village of

4km Agés (221/488)

Path joins main street. Follow this past *fountain* (R) and follow street through village. Continue on road to

2km Atapuerco (223/486)

Two fountains, bar panadería. Fortress-like church uphill on R.

Turn L just before bar(R), diagonally off road and then veer further L to UMUR. KSO uphill *(good views)*, ignoring turning to R and enter a wide ravine. *NB: Don't stray from the footpath - there is a military firing range in this area!*

Fork R at clearing in ravine between piles of cairns. KSO, following path as it winds its way to the top *(waymarks on ground in this section)*, veering L to a <u>very</u> large wooden cross, nearly 30ft high, just after crossing another track at right angles (alt. 1,070m). *Panoramic views - to Burgos on a clear day and view over the other villages you will pass through on the way there, like a map. Burgos is farther away than it looks from here though - at least 5 hours on foot to the city centre.*

Go downhill, veering R at first, then L at crossing of similar paths *(arrows on ground)*. FP joins track from R. KSO downhill. [RJ: flashes on rocks at L <u>before</u> small R turn.]

Cross track and KSO downhill through shallow valley, along its floor. Shortly before the village ahead of you the track joins one coming from the L. *(Telephone aerials up on hill to R.)* Turn L when you reach the road and enter village of

4km Cardeñuela (227/482)

Bar.

KSO through village and continue on road, ignoring turns to L and R to

2km Orbaneja (229/480)

Burgos. Arco de Santa María

KSO. Cross motorway and KSO on road for 2km till you reach the railway line (Madrid-Irún), // to it. Follow road round (rubbish tip on L) to cross bridge over the railway. Then: either follow road till it joins the N1 after 100m or turn R at bend in road immediately after bridge and go down lane to church of

4km Villafría (233/476)
Now a suburb of Burgos. Two bars near church (whose tower has a complex arrangement of "accommodation" for the storks), shop. Several bars on main road, hostal, bar with rooms, restaurant. Frequent bus service to

Burgos.

Continue on N1 into Burgos - *7km of heavy lorries, fast cars, buses - the worst section of the whole camino.* KSO along the main road towards the city centre. After 4-5km and a large crossing the road becomes the *Calle Vitoria.* When you get to another large junction (traffic divides R for Santander, centre for city and L to Madrid) you can either continue along the *Calle Vitoria* into the centre of Burgos or take a road // to it on the L, along the river and shaded, the *Avenida General Sanjurio.* This becomes the pedestrianised *Paseo de Espolón* in the city centre.

7km Burgos 856m (240/469)

Population 170,000. All facilities. RENFE. Buses to Pamplona, Logroño, Madrid etc.

Capital of Castille and end of the fifth stage in Aymery Picaud's guide. A place to spend at least a whole day. Gothic cathedral with Santiago chapel, many other important buildings, including the Gothic church of San Nicolás and, just outside the town, the monastery of Las Huelgas with its church, very fine Romanesque cloisters, chapel of Santiago and museum and the Hospital del Rey, a resting place for sick or tired pilgrims.

To leave Burgos turn L at the end of the *Calle Vitoria* to the *Paseo de Espolón* if you have not already done so and continue along the river on the *Avenida del Generalissimo*, the *Paseo de la Isla*, the *Paseo Fuente* and cross the river by the *Puente Malatos (the last one before the railway bridge).* Turn R on the other side along the main road past the *Hospital del Rey (now restored as part of the University's Law Faculty).* Weighbridge (bascula municipal).

After 3km, at traffic lights opposite the *Mesón Restaurante Bellavista*, the main road veers L. Fork R down a minor road *(tree-lined).* At the end (0.5km) KSO along a farm track (// to railway line to L) past fields, a tree plantation and more fields. KSO ignoring turns to L and R. After 3km reach

6km Villabilla de Burgos 837m (247/462)

Church (L) on other side of railway line. Cross minor/branch line but not the main (Madrid-Irún) line. Fork R, passing to the L of a house in front of a flour factory (R). Follow the road round to the R, cross a bridge over a river and turn L on other side, past two bridges onto a farm road through fields. *(Main road ahead to L.)* KSO for 1km till you reach the road. Turn L along it, cross to other side, and cross bridge over the River *Arlanzón*.

After bridge fork L down a track // to main road and continue on it until it joins the road at entry to

4km Tardájos 828m (250/459)
Shops, bars, restaurant, fonda.

Pass rollo on L on entry. Fork L opposite bar down *Calle del Mediodía*. Turn R at end and then L on to a minor road. KSO to

1.5km Rabé de las Calzadas (251.5/457.5)
Fountain.

KSO through village and turn R in a triangular "square". KSO. Fork R at modern chapel (L) by cemetery (L) then fork L 50m further on.

Track joins from R and the path levels out to a vast, seemingly endless plateau. This is the "meseta", lush and green in spring, a dustbowl in summer. Depending on your preferences you will either find it extremely tedious or, if you like undulating expanses reaching out to infinity in all directions, hauntingly beautiful, especially in the early morning light. Although it is so far removed from the noise of "civilisation" it is far from silent, as it now becomes obvious quite how much sound the wind, the insects, the birds and the grass actually make.

500m further on path descends to a valley (approx. 1.5km to village ahead). Join UMUR coming from R. When you get to the road cross it and enter village of

8.5km Hornillos del Camino (260/449)
Small village with a large Gothic church, formerly an important pilgrim halt with a hospital and a small Benedictine monastery.

Continue to the end of the village *(no shops or bars)* and turn R at the public weighbridge. Turn L after 1km and fork R (ie. keeping straight on) 500m further on. Fork R again after 10m, uphill all the time. Turn L at next junction.

At the top of the hill and beginning of the plateau cross a track and KSO. *Apart from electricity pylons in the distance to the L there is no sign of any sort of habitation at all in any direction, giving a feeling of being on the roof of the world.* KSO at next two junctions (first is a cross roads), second a T junction to L).

Cross a UMUR and KSO. Shortly afterwards track descends to valley. Keep R at fork. Cross another UMUR (ruined houses to L and R) and KSO uphill again. Turn L at next fork (ie. straight on) and then the path levels out again. *Nothing in sight for miles and miles around.*

Cross a minor road and KSO (two large clumps of trees away to R in distance). Cross grassy track and KSO. Cross another track and KSO again.

2km past the last minor road a valley suddenly appears on your R. KSO. 500m later another valley appears ahead and just after that another path joins from behind L. Then - all of a sudden - the church and village of *Hontanas* appears below you. Go down the path into the village, following the path to the R and then to the L down the main street. *Fountain* (L) and church (L).

11km Hontanas 870m (271/438)

Pilgrim village (it's name means "the fountains") dominated by its church.
Fountain. Swimming pool with bar (summer).

Continue past fountain (L), church (L), weighbridge (R) and swimming pool (R). When you get to the road the waymarks direct you to cross it and fork R (ie. to L before you've crossed over) along a track on the other side. However, although this takes you off the road, // to it, there is hardly any shade at all and you may prefer, instead, to stay on the road as it has very little traffic and is tree-lined almost all the way to Castrojeriz.

Otherwise, after crossing the road, turn L 300m further on, at a junction after three large trees. When you reach the ruins of the **Molino del Cubo** take the upper path (ie. keep your height) and KSO, uphill slightly, to the ruin of *San Miguel*. Pass below it. The track then descends to join another from the R. Fork L. 10m later a track joins from behind L - KSO (still // to road). KSO at next fork. Track then veers L to join road. Follow it for 1km to the ruins of

4km Hospital San Anton (275/434)

Gothic hospital founded by the Antonianos, a French order believed to possess powers of healing Saint Anthony's Fire, a type of gangrene which

appeared in Europe in the tenth century. Pilgrims came here in search of a cure and were sent on their way after a blessing with the "Tau" (T-shaped) cross. The remains are on both sides of the road, which passes under an archway. Bread for pilgrims was placed in a niche to be seen on the left of the road.

Continue along tree-lined road *(ruins of alcázar on hill above town visible ahead)* to

3km Castrojeriz 800m (278/431)
Pop. 1185. Shops, bars, restaurant, bank. Hostal, campsite.

Town built by the Romans and an important stopping place for pilgrims in former times: there were still seven hospitals left at the beginning of the nineteenth century. Collegiate church of Nuestra Señora de la Manzana (thirteenth- and seventeenth-century with statue of Saint James), church of San Juan (interesting cloister), church of San Domingo (with small museum).

Colegiata de Nuestra Señora de la Manzano, Castrojeriz

MAP 5

N >

Grañeras • • El Burgo Ranero

Bercianos • • Calzadilla
de los
Hermanillos

Calzada del Coto •

SAHAGÚN • R. CEA

LEÓN

C 611 R. VALDELARADUEY

• San Nicolás del
Real Camino

Moratinos • • Lágartos

Terradillos de los
Templarios

• Ledigos

PALENCIA

P 972 • Calzadilla de la Cueva

N 120

Cervatos de la Cueva • • Bustillo del Páramo
de Carrión

R. CUEZA

C 615

• Villotilla

R. CARRIÓN

← PALENCIA C 615 • CARRION DE LAS CONDES

P 980 R. UCIEZA

• Villálcazar de Sirga

Villamentero de Campos • • Arconada
Revenga de Campos • • Villovieco

N 611
PALENCIA • Población del Campo

P 981

N 120

FROMISTA

N 611

P 431

• Boadilla del Camino

P 432

CANAL DE
CASTILLA

Itero de la Vega •

R. PISURGA

Turn R at entrance to Castrojeriz to *N-S de la Manzana (worth a visit)* and then turn L through village (very long). To leave, pass church of *San Juan* (R) and go down to road. Veer L to cross roads. Turn L, cross road and after 50m turn L down a UMUR. After 1.5km cross bridge over *Río Odrilla* and shortly afterwards *(house visible away to L)*, at staggered junction, KSO up path that winds its way, veering L, uphill to the top of the hill and the monument you can see on the skyline. You are back on the meseta again (1km from bridge). At the top KSO (ie. don't turn L) towards iron crosses (waymarks).

KSO, following these waymarks *(crosses with yellow plastic on them)* and shortly afterwards, after approx. 500m you look down to a huge valley (bowl-like) below you. *Panoramic views.* From here the path leads more or less straight ahead to *Itero de lCastillo* (though it doesn't actually go into the village).

Descend on track through fields for 1-2km. Cross a farm road and KSO. Fork L slightly downhill when track divides. Cross another farm road and KSO and approx. 1km afterwards join a minor road, going slightly uphill, at the **Fuente del Piojo** *(fountain)*.

Turn R along road for 1km to crossroads. *(Itero de la Vega visible ahead.)* Turn L along road (ignore farm track back to L). Pass *Ermita San Nicolas* (l) and then cross bridge over *Río Pisuerga* - the boundary between the provinces of Burgos and Palencia. *(The 65km stretch of the camino which passes through Palencia is particularly rich in historic monuments.)* Fork R on other side of bridge down minor road for 1.5km to village of

10km Itero de la Vega (288/421)
Shop.

Thirteenth-century Ermita de la Piedad (with statue of Saint James the Pilgrim) at entrance to village, sixteenth-century church of San Pedro.

KSO through village *(Calle Conde Vallellano, Calle Santa María)* cross end of main square *(fountain, rollo)*. Continue straight on and then turn L down *Calle Marqués de Estrella*, following white arrows painted on road. Turn R into *Calle Commandante Ramirez*. Pass five large trees (L) *(another fountain)* and KSO to crossroads.

Cross road and continue along UMUR flanked by water channels on either side. Pass turning (L) to hamlet of **Bodegas** after 1km and KSO. Cross bridge over *Canal Pisuerga* and continue straight on to top of hill (three humps visible ahead on skyline). View of Boadilla del Camino (3km ahead) at the top.

Cross canal and turn R along bank. Then either follow street round to R to leave village or head for church to enter it. [RJ: fork R at fountain.]

8km Boadilla del Camino 782m (296/413)
Bar/shop. Fifteenth-century rollo.

To leave continue past bar and then turn L alongside football ground (R) and L again past warehouse along UMUR. KSO. Go through a gap in the irrigation channels (raised up) and 200m further on fork R up a bank to join the towpath of the *Canal de Castilla.* KSO along it for 3km. Cross the footbridge over the canal by a lock, veer R down a FP down a bank, go along a tree-lined path for 100m and turn R onto road. Follow it, veering L under railway bridge to crossroads (by *Tourist Office*). [RJ: follow signs for "Astadillo" to bend in road (to R) and then cross canal at footbridge.]

5km Fromista 780m (301/408)
Population 1400. All facilities. RENFE.

End of the sixth stage in Aimery Picaud's guide. Small town with Romanesque church of San Martín, a National Monument, and one of the best preserved of the whole camino. It has 315 carved figures of animals, humans (some humorous), flowers, monsters etc. in a line round the church under the eaves, all in perfect condition. Church of Santa María del Castillo (also a National Monument), erected on the site of an ancient fortress, has an altarpiece with twenty-nine paintings. Fifteenth-century church of San Pedro, Ermita del Otero.

To leave - KSO along road to Carrión de las Condes (ie. cross road at cross roads by Tourist Office) and continue for 4km (*rollo at side of road*). Chapel at Km16 post.

4km Población de Campos 790m (305/404)
2 bars, shop (unmarked).

Small village with the remains of a former pilgrim hospital, Ermita del Socorro and thirteenth-century Ermita de San Miguel (both thirteenth-century), seventeenth-century church of the Magdelena, Fuente San Miguel L near cemetery.

Fork R up concrete road *(paseo del Cementerio)* to visit village, aiming for church. At junction behind church take minor road ahead with raised irrigation channel down LH side. Otherwise, turn L past village, join above road and turn L.

KSO. After 3km pass a *fountain on RH side, built in 1989, with a wayside cross, shell and red/white cross motif.* KSO to

3km Villovieco 790m (308/401)

Turn L over bridge over the River *Ucieza* and then immediately R along its bank and KSO. Follow the bank for 5km, as far as the **Ermita de la Virgen del Río** *(contains alabaster statue of Saint James the pilgrim). Sometimes it is necessary to cross small irrigation channels running at right angles to the river - some have stepping stones - and then go back onto the path again. The last km is fairly shady.*

Turn L along the road when you reach the *ermita (a large building, similar to a church)* which is near a bridge. Then pass the *Ermita del Cristo de la Salud (small - still in use)* (L) and after 1km enter

6km Villalcazar de Sirga 809m (314/395)

Bar, two mesóns (no shop), fountain in public garden.

Also known as "Villasirga". The village is dominated by the thirteenth-century church of Santa María la Blanca, a National Monument, with very fine portals, chapel of Santiago with tombs and statues, including one of Saint James, all in a very fine state of preservation and well worth a visit.

Turn R to enter village. Otherwise KSO to main road. Turn R and continue along it, *with cornfields to both sides in an undulating landscape. This road is not usually too busy but there is <u>no shade at all</u>. Bodegas in fields to side of road.*

6km Carrión de las Condes 840m (320/389)

Population 2800. All facilities. Campsite near river. Churches of Santa María del Camino (or de la Victoria), Santiago (splendid portal, church burnt in 1809 War of Independence), Monastery of San Zoilo (National Monument) with sixteenth-century cloisters, Convento de Santa Clara and museum. To enter town - turn L off road at flour factory. To leave - continue past square and church of *Santa María* and turn R. Pass in front of church of *Santiago* and veer L to cross the River *Carrión* by the main bridge. Pass in front of the *Monastery of San Zoilo* (L) and

71

come to a large crossroads 300m later. KSO for 300m further, past a petrol station, to another crossroads where the N120 veers L. KSO along a minor road which is signposted to "Villotilla 6". KSO for 4km.

Pass the *Abadía de Benvívere (R), former abbey but now a private house,* just before a sharp bend in the road where a bridge crosses a small river. 300m metres after the bridge there is a junction with a minor road: cross it and KSO along a farm road *(scallop shell waymark)* through cornfields. *The landscape is flat in all directions.*

KSO for 2.5km to plantation of "chopos" (poplars, R) and road. Cross it, KSO for 6km, ignoring turnings to L and R. *The church tower and cemetery are visible to the R shortly* before you enter the village of

17km Calzadilla de la Cueva (337/372)
Bar/restaurant (has rooms). Shaded area with seats at end of village (R).
Continue straight on through village to road. Cross the River *Cueza* and KSO on the road, passing the remains of the *eleventh-century pilgrim hospital,* formerly very important, of

2km Santa María de las Tiendas (339/370)
From here the landscape becomes less flat and slightly undulating. Woods to L and R, away from road. Mountains in distance to R.
Continue on main road to

4km Ledigos 883m (343/366)
Bar, shop.
Church of Santiago with a statue of Saint James.
At entrance to village fork R off road. Continue through village and then turn R to join main road again, crossing the River *Cueza* again. KSO on road.

4km Terradillos de los Templarios (347/362)
Shop, fonda.
Eighteenth-century church of San Pedro.
Continue on the main road, passing turnings to the L to *Moratinos* and then *San Nicolás del Real Camino (fountain),* after which you leave the province of Palencia to enter León. *There is a fair amount of traffic on this stretch (but less on Sundays, when there are no heavy goods*

vehicles) and the stretch from Calzadilla de la Cueza to Sahagún can therefore be rather tedious. Sahagún is now visible ahead.

After this you can either (a) continue along the road for 7km more, directly to Sahagún, turning off the N120 at the flour mill or (b) turn R off the road, shortly after the provincial boundary, onto a track. Turn L along a clear track which now runs // to main road. KSO through fields, ignoring turnings to L and R. *Panoramic views.* Then, at a large rubbish tip (probably smoking), another track joins from the R. Here you can either turn L and return to the road again at Km235 (*and in which case you will simply have done a "rodeo" to get away from the traffic for a while, admire the view and perhaps have a quiet sit down*) or KSO downhill, aiming for the River *Valdelaraduey* at the bottom, opposite the **Ermita Virgen del Puente** on the other side (*a former pilgrim hospice*). This is the old route. There is no longer a bridge at this point but as the river is extremely shallow here (only a few inches deep) it should normally be possible to cross it.

(If you rejoined the road again after the rubbish tip KSO on road until after you have crossed the road bridge over the *Valderaduey*. Turn R immediately along a track along the river bank for 100m until you reach the *Ermita, a former pilgrim hospice. Trees and a good place for a rest.*)

The path leading from here into Sahagún is still known as the *Camino Francés de la Virgen.* Turn L at the *Ermita* and follow the path until you reach the embankment of the Sahagún bypass. Turn L under bridge and KSO on other side, aiming for a very large white grain silo ahead. When you get there, cross the N120 and enter

11km Sahagún 816m (358/351)

Population 2,700. All facilities. RENFE on León-Palencia line, campsite, swimming pool. Tourist Office.

End of the seventh stage in Aimery Picaud's guide. Sahagún takes its name from a contraction of San Fagún or Facondo, a Roman martyr. A monastery was founded here as early as 904 and then, in 1080, the order of Cluny established itself and Sahagún became the foremost Benedictine abbey in Spain. Nothing remains of the five pilgrim hospitals founded in the eleventh century but there are several churches of outstanding architectural merit: San Tirso, San Lorenzo and La Peregrina (all three national Monuments), San Juan de Sahagún, La Trinidad and, 5km to the south, San Pedro de las Dueñas (also a National Monument).

After crossing the main road continue down a small street (*Calle Ronda Estación*). As you approach the railway line (with the station on your L) follow it for a short distance and then cross it at the bridge. KSO down the *Calle José Antonio*, the *Calle del Peso* (fork R after this for the town centre), the *Calle Rua* and the *Calle de las Monjas*. At the end you will come to an open space, with the *Convent of the Madres Benedictinas* and the museum of religious painting on your R. (Turn R here for the *Arco de San Benito* and the church of *San Tirso*.)

To leave Sahagún continue straight from the *Calle de las Monjas* along the *Calle de Rey Don Antonio* and out of the town across the bridge over the River *Cea. This is bordered with poplar trees and legend has it that at a time when both Moors and Christians were battling for control of northern Spain a Christian force camped near Sahagún. Before retiring for the night some of the men stuck their lances in the ground and woke up the following morning to find that they had sprouted roots, branches and leaves.* Pass the swimming pool (R) and follow the main road to León to

6km Calzada del Coto (364/345)

Leave the road here along a turning to the R. *At this point the Camino divides, the two paths running more or less parallel to each other with the railway line in between them for much of the way, merging when they reach Mansilla de las Mulas.*

A. Calzada de los Peregrinos

This is an old Roman road, the Vía Trajana, but is very isolated and there is little or no water, no accommodation, no shops or bars and virtually no shade from the sun for 30kms. It is definitely not recommended in July or August but for fit walkers who like space, silence and unlimited solitude it is perhaps the more attractive of the two routes at other times, provided you carry plenty of food and water and set out very early in the morning. There are not many waymarks on this route but it is easy to follow as there are few turnings to make and, like most of the rest of the camino, you are always walking in a straight line due west.

Turn R into the village of *Calzada del Coto (shop)* past the *Ermita de San Roque* on your R and follow the street through the village. At the end ignore the track to the L *(this leads to Bercianos)* and KSO(R). After 2km cross the bridge over the railway line *(artificial lake to L on other side)* and KSO.

After this you enter a wooded area, going gradually uphill. Small, scrubby trees and a little shade. After 3km (from the railway bridge) and just before you leave the woods pass the *Granja Valdelocajos*, a large farm with modern houses and some very large *dogs* (probably loose!). 1km further on, on your R, is the newly installed *Fuente de los Peregrinos* and a picnic area. KSO for 3km till you reach

9km Calzadilla de los Hermanos

Enter the village and KSO along the main street, past the *ermita* (L) and continue to the end where a road joins from behind R.

Continue on the road *across an immense plateau stretching to the horizon on all sides. From time to time you can see the poles along the railway line away to the L and the grain silo at El Burgo Ranero and you may see/hear a train in the distance but otherwise all you can see around you are the cornfields seemingly reaching away to infinity.*

After 3.5km you will come to a junction where the camino ceases to be tarred and continues as an UMUR, on the other side of the tarred road that crosses it *(L to El Burgo Ranbero, R to Villamartín de D. Sancho)*. KSO for 13.5km, ignoring any turnings you may see to L and R, until you reach the deserted railway station at

17km Apeadero Villamarco

Trains do in fact still stop here, though presumably only on request.

Do not cross the railway line at the station *(the road on the other side leads to the village of Villamarco, some 2km to the south)* but KSO more or less // to it. After 4km you will pass through the valleys of 2 dried up rivers and from time to time you will see tracks leading off to L and R. KSO. After a further 6km you will enter 2 more river valleys - the path veers L here: follow it and KSO. 200m after emerging from the second valley there is a junction: KSO and the church tower of *Reliegos* is suddenly visible ahead. If you want to go there *(bar)* and finish by the Real Camino Francés KSO (you are about 500m away from it). Otherwise - turn R down a track shortly after the junction. Go downhill along a track in a straight line for 6km until you reach *Mansilla de las Mulas* (and which you will have seen ahead of you in the distance since nearing Reliegos). Enter the town by a canal and turn L along the main road. KSO at junction, enter town and KSO along main street.

B. Camino Real Frances

This route passes to the south of the other one, though leading directly west. At the point where you turn off the main road from Sahagún towards Calzada del Coto do <u>not</u> enter the village but take the L turn along an UMUR lined with newly planted trees. *This is the road to Bercianos and is used by quite a lot of vehicles, even though it is not (yet) tarred, which send up huge clouds of dust in the dry summer months.* Pass a laguna (R) after 1.7km and then, after 2km, the *Ermita de Perales* (L). KSO. After 1km and after crossing the bridge over the River *Coso* (probably dry) enter the village of

5km Bercianos del Real Camino (369/340)

Bar, shop.

   Church of El Salvador.

   Follow the main road through the village. In the distance you will see the silos of *El Burgo Ranero*, 7km away. *It was in between these two places that the seventeenth-century Italian pilgrim Domenico Laffi came across the body of a fellow pilgrim who had been attacked by wolves - this was one of the loneliest stretches of the entire pilgrimage, as it still is today.* Continue directly west along the well-defined track until you reach the village of

7km El Burgo Ranero (376/333)

Shop, bar/restaurant, fonda.

   Follow the main road through the village past the church (R), cross a road that intersects the village from north to south and past the cemetery (L). *2km further on on the L is a group of ten trees (which you will see before you get to them) with a brick fountain set back from the road - a good place for a rest.* KSO.

   The road carries straight on, and after 6km passes a turning, on the L, to the village of *Villamarco* (the village itself is 1km off route).

   2km further on the route crosses the railway line and continues with this to its left for a while. The route is still well-waymarked with yellow arrows. It enters a small valley, crossing first the

"River" *Valdearcos* and then, 1km further on, the "River" *Santa María* (usually dried up). *Shortly after this there is another shaded area with trees and the landscape becomes less flat, with bodegas (storage cellars for keeping wine cool) set into the hilly ground at intervals.* 2km further on enter

12km Reliegos (388/321)

Bar.

KSO through village and out the other side on a stony track across a plain, where you will see *Mansilla de las Mulas* 6km away in the distance. Continue west until you reach the main road, cross it and the bridge over the canal and enter the town.

6km Mansilla de las Mulas 799m (394/315)

Population 1,800. Shops, bars, restaurant, hostal, campsite.

Substantial remains of the twelfth-century town walls. Thirteenth-century church of Santa María, Capilla Nuestra Señora de Gracia.

Continue along the main street to the end of the town and cross the bridge over the River Esla. Fork L onto the old road and then onto a track which continues // to the main road, apart from a few exceptions, for 5km until you reach the village of

6km Puente Villarente (400/309)

Shops, bars, restaurant, hostal.

Small village with a twenty-arch bridge over the River Porma.

After this the camino follows the main road (with a <u>lot</u> of traffic) all the way to León. At the petrol station to the R on leaving Puente Villarente a path is waymarked to the R but is hard to follow, although, in theory, it is supposed to go as far as **Valdelafuente** *(bar, farmacía)* before it joins the road again.

As you approach León fork L as road veers R at *Avenida de Madrid*. Cross the River *Torío* at *Puente Castro* (by the footbridge). Pass the Red Cross HQ (L) and KSO to roundabout with fountains playing amidst very modern sculptures. Cross road and veer R along *Calle Santa Ana* (at the back of church of same name) into the centre of León and the cathedral via the *Calle Barahona, Calle Puertamoneda*, past the church of *Santa María del Mercado* (R), and the *Calle de la Rua*.

11km León 822m (411/298)

Population 135,000. All facilities. Youth Hostel. RENFE. Buses to all major towns. Tourist office opposite Cathedral.

End of the eighth stage in Aimery Picaud's guide and another place worth spending a whole day. The three most important monuments are the

thirteenth-century Cathedral in French Gothic style with superb stained glass windows, the Basilica of San Isidoro containing the Royal Pantheon (with twelfth-century wall and ceiling paintings) and a fine Romanesque church and San Marcos, formerly an important pilgrim hospital (now a Parador). León also contains one of the few Gaudí buildings outside Barcelona - the Casa de las Bottines, once a private house but now a bank.

To leave León - cross bridge over *Río Bernesga* by the *Hotel San Marcos*. KSO past public garden (R) and continue along this road, crossing the railway line, until you reach the *Iglesia Capilla de Santiago* (R). Turn L after the church along the *Calle Doña Sira Sampedro* and then cross the waste land to return to the road again. Turn L, cross the road and then turn R after a few yards and go uphill past "bodegas" (R). Pass R between buildings and factory *(Calle de la Orma)*. KSO alongside long wall. Pass rubbish tip (L). KSO behind factory and then veer R uphill. At top KSO. *(This may sound complicated but all you are doing is playing hide and seek with the main road, avoiding it where possible.)*

KSO(L) at fork. When you get to some houses veer L to church (modern) of *Virgen del Camino (its tower is visible from a distance as it is <u>very</u> tall).* Turn L to main road at

6km Virgen del Camino 905m (417/292)
Small town with shops, bars, restaurant, hostal.

Church of San Froilan (modern) has a very interesting façade which includes thirteen huge bronze statues, one of which is Saint James pointing the way to Santiago. Its interior is very plain apart from an extremely ornate baroque reredos, retained from a former church on this site.

In the next section you basically follow the road but often take parallel tracks to avoid actually walking along it.

50m after the church turn L down a track leading to the cemetery. Go up hill past cemetery (L) and rejoin road in front of a factory. Continue on path above road (L) - ahead you can see a (complicated) motorway junction.

When you rejoin the road cross the first part (a slip road) carefully, crossing where you see the yellow arrows painted on the road itself, and walk on the hard shoulder of the main Madrid-Astorga road. KSO, go under <u>both</u> bridges and KSO. Continue along the road.

3km Valverde de la Virgen 887m (420/289)
Bar, fuente.

2km San Miguel del Camino (422/287)
Shortly after San Miguel fork L off road onto track // to it. Veer R at farm and follow track across open land more or less // to road. When you think you are going to rejoin the road KSO instead down dip to track // to road. KSO.

6km Urbanización de Santiago (428/281)
Continue on road to

2km Villadangos del Páramo (430/279)
Shops, bars, fonda, pharmacy, restaurant.

Originally a Roman town. Church of Santiago has a painting of Santiago Matamoros in its main altarpiece. (The word "páramo" in this and many other place names means "bleak plateau".)

Cross road at entrance to village, fork R and enter village. Turn L at end to return to main road for a short while. Then fork L off it onto a track // to road. Follow this for as far as is practicable and then rejoin road to walk on hard shoulder. *Unfortunately there is no alternative in this section as all the land to L and R of the road is criss-crossed with canals, dykes and deep irrigation channels.* Continue to

4km San Martín del Camino (434/275)
Small shop, 2 bars.

KSO and shortly outside village cross road and fork R onto track // to road. At farm veer slightly R to pass it (on your L) then veer L again to follow track // to road. KSO until, after 2km, the track forks away from the road. Turn L, cross bridge over dyke and return to road over crash barrier.

KSO. 1.5km before *Hospital de Orbigo*, opposite a gravel works, turn R down a lane. Follow path through fields to

7km Hospital de Orbigo 819m (441/268)
Small town, population 1320, with shops, fonda, restaurant, campsite, two fountains.

The longest pilgrim bridge in Spain, crossing the River Orbigo. It is

204 metres long and has twenty arches. It is known as the bridge of the Paso Honroso in memory of a month long jousting tournament which took place in 1434, breaking 300 lances and leaving one person dead. Its champions continued to Santiago where they left a golden necklace on the processional statue of Santiago Menor (reportedly still there).

Cross Roman bridge and continue past church of *Santa María* (R) down main street to end of town (down the *Calle Camino de Santiago*). At the cross roads with an UMUR at the end you can either
a) KSO (waymarked) to continue on the road route to Astorga or
b) (also waymarked) turn R for an alternative country route as far as San Justo de la Vega (the one described here).

KSO along minor road to

2km Villares de Orbigo 919m (443/266)

Ignore turns to L and R. Enter village, turn L then R, then veer R (past lavadero). KSO. Turn R onto road, cross it and KSO. After 200m turn L up junction with green lane. KSO for 1km and join road again. Turn R to village of

1km Santibañez de Valdeiglesias 845m (444/265)

Turn L at next junction (ie. straight on). Enter village, follow main street, turn R at *fountain* (ie. do not go as far as the church). Turn R uphill and KSO. Fork L downhill at fork. After 300m fork R at next fork. KSO uphill. Enter woods [RJ: take R fork just before village].

Turn R at next fork (ie. straight on) and L at next. At top of hill turn R to newly cut out road. Follow it down to crossroads at bottom. KSO to shaded track then follow it uphill along side of fields (R). *Fields both sides then woods both sides.* Go downhill past grove of trees (L) and remains of wall.

KSO uphill in straight line to farm building (R) at top, with small wood slightly ahead. At junction of tracks take second L turn which leads after 500m to the *Crucero de Santo Toribio (and splendid views of Astorga). (Toribio, along with Genadio, both from Astorga, Isidore of Seville and Ildefonso of Toledo, was one of the four bishop saints.)* Turn R downhill, join main road at bend (crash barrier) and KSO to village of

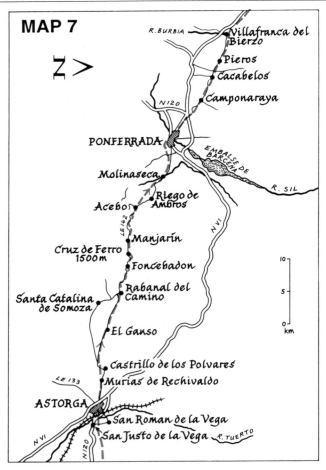

MAP 7

N >

R. BURBIA — Villafranca del Bierzo

Pieros

Cacabelos

Camponaraya

N120

PONFERRADA

EMBALSE DE BARCENA

Molinaseca

R. SIL

Riego de Ambros

Acebo

LE 142

Manjarín

Cruz de Ferro 1500 m

Foncebadon

Rabanal del Camino

Santa Catalina de Somoza

N VI

El Ganso

10

5

0
km

Castrillo de los Polvares

LE 133

Murias de Rechivaldo

ASTORGA

San Roman de la Vega

N VI

N120

San Justo de la Vega R. TUERTO

9km San Justo de la Vega (453/256)
Bars, shop, hostal.
   Church with old tower but very modern windows and brick nave.
   Continue through village and out along main road until you
have crossed the road bridge over the River *Tuerto*. Turn R then L

along a shaded lane // to the road. Follow this for 2km past field, factory and another field until you cross a bridge over a small canal. Turn L and KSO to main road, arriving just before a level crossing. Turn R along this road, cross two level crossings and follow road uphill into town. Turn R to visit cathedral.

5km Astorga 869m (458/251)

Population 14,000, all facilities. RENFE. Buses to León and Villafranca del Bierzo. Tourist Office opposite Cathedral.

A town dating from Roman times, with extensive remains of its original town walls behind the Cathedral. Astorga was (and still is) the junction of two pilgrim routes, the <u>camino francés</u> (described here) and the <u>camino mozárabe</u> or <u>Vía de la Plata</u>. This explains the unusually large number of pilgrim hospitals formerly in existence (there were twenty-two in the Middle Ages), the last of which, the Hospital de las Cinco Llagas (the Five Wounds) was burned down earlier this century. Gothic Cathedral with interesting choir stalls and museum, Bishop's Palace built by the Catalan architect Antonio Gaudí, with pilgrim museum. Several other interesting churches, Baroque town hall. It is worth spending at least half a day here.

Between Astorga and Ponferrada the camino passes through the isolated area of the Maragatería (as far as the Cruz de Ferro) and then into the Bierzo, which continues until you leave the province of León and enter Galicia. For many people this is one of the most beautiful stretches of the camino, most of it in the Montes de León, but as there are few villages and few bars or shops along the way it is advisable to carry a certain amount of food and water. Since the route is also quite high (the Cruz de Ferro is at1,504m) warm clothing is needed, even in summer.

Much of the camino between Astorga and Molinaseca is in fact on the road but it is very quiet and there is very little traffic.

To leave Astorga - turn L at traffic lights on main road out of Astorga to the west onto minor road signposted "Santa Colomba de Somoza" and "Castrillo de los Polvazares". KSO to *Valdeviejas*, passing a memorial sign (L) to "peregrinos identes" and then an old people's complex (L). Pass the *Ermita Ecco Homo* (L) and then either KSO on road itself or along a track beside it as far as the bridge over the River *Jerga* and then return to the road. Continue to village of

5km Murias de Rechivaldo 882m (463/246)
Mesón.

Fork L onto a track between two trees just past the village name sign and pass along to the side of the village to its L. Enter street (*"Camino de Santiago"*) and continue along to the end, when it becomes a track leading to open country.

[*1km further on a short detour is recommended to* **Castrillo de los Polvazares**, *a cobbled village typical of the Maragatería which is a National Monument and in a very fine state of preservation. To leave you will have to retrace your steps (1km) as the road into the village is a dead end.*]

Follow this track straight on for 2km, until you reach the road at a junction. Fork R here along a road signposted "El Ganso 5" and KSO to village of

5km Santa Catalina de Somoza 977m (468/241)
Fork R at entrance to village along lane towards church and KSO along *Calle Real*. Rejoin road at large green wooden wayside cross and KSO along road to

5km El Ganso 1,020m (473/236)
Small village which formerly had a monastery and pilgrim hospital. Church of Santiago, with chapel of "Cristo de los Peregrinos".

Fork R at entrance to village along lane (village to your L). KSO and then turn L back onto road at church. KSO along road, pass a turning to "Rabanal Viejo" after 3km, at the *Puente Pañote*, and continue to

6km Rabanal del Camino 1,149m (479/230)
Two bars (meals available at both), fountain.

End of the ninth stage in Aimery Picaud's guide. Ermita del Santo Cristo at entrance to village, church of San José and parish church of Santa María. Today the population is only forty-two, except in summer when migrants return for their holidays, but in former times it was an important pilgrim halt and considerably larger, as the presence of three churches testifies.

Turn R off road after church (L) to enter village. Pass churches of *San José* and *Santa María* and mesón and KSO along green lane for

1km to rejoin road again. Fork L along it. *(Fountain to R of road after 2km at KM post 25, with icy cold water.)* Continue to climb and KSO to village of

5km Foncebadón 1495m (484/225)
Today this village is almost abandoned but in the twelfth century the hermit Gaucelmo built a church, hospital and hospice for pilgrims, of which the remains still exist. Fountain above track to R.

Fork L off road, enter village and continue to end. KSO, passing ruined church and rejoin road after 1km. Turn L and 300m further on reach the

1km Cruz de Ferro 1504m (485/224)
A very tall iron cross atop a huge cairn. Traditionally pilgrims brought a stone with them from home to add to the pile. Fantastic views on a clear day, with Monte Teleno over in the distance to the south. Modern Ermita de Santiago. From here the route is almost all downhill to Ponferrada, some 25km.

[RJ: turn R off road at 22nd snow pole on road after passing the cross. If you miss it, continue along the road to rejoin the camino at the entrance to Foncebadón.]

KSO on road, passing highest point of the entire route (at 1517m) to abandoned village of

3km Manjarín 1,451m (488/221)
Fountain on L on leaving village.

Continue on road for 2km, pass turning to military base *(visible on hill above road, with radar, etc.)* and KSO.

Mountain ranges visible ahead of you and to the L.

After 1-2km watch out for a turning off the road to the L; this shortcuts some of the road's many "hairpins." However, if you miss it don't worry but do watch out for the next turning, R, off the road, which climbs up between two small hills; this cuts off quite a long section of the road, which you rejoin on the other side *(good view of Ponferrada ahead).* [RJ: turn L uphill, near drain, before road veers R.]

2km further on fork L off road onto FP going downhill below the road (which remains on your R). Continue along it, descending steeply, until below you, abruptly, you reach the slate-roofed

village of

9km El Acebo 1.156m (497/212)

Fountain on roadside as you leave the FP and two others in village. Bar.

Another village which formerly had a pilgrim hospital, a single long, narrow street whose old houses have overhanging balconies at first floor level and outside staircases. Their slate roofs are a sudden change from the red pantiles encountered up to now. Church has statue of Santiago Peregrino.

KSO through village, past *Ermita and cemetery and a memorial in the form of an iron bicycle sculpture to a German pilgrim killed there whilst cycling to Santiago in 1987.* Continue on road. 1km before the next village of *Riego de Ambrós*, visible ahead, watch out for a turning to L off road at a bend *(stone hut to R of road, beyond the turning)* onto a FP below the road. Follow this [after a while another track joins from back R].

In the section from Foncebadón to Riego de Ambrós there are a lot of

View of El Acebo

wayside crosses with scallop shells below: memorials to pilgrims who died en route?

2km Riego de Ambrós 920m (499/210)
Two bars, shop, fountain.

Enter village, follow street straight on (downhill all the time) and then turn R down a grassy lane. Continue downhill through trees for 1km (in a straight line all the time), then join a farm track. Join a road a few metres further on and turn L along it. 80m after this turn R off the road to a track. KSO then fork R downhill and zigzag down to clearing in a wood with enormous chestnut trees. KSO downhill.

After a while, although the path remains level, the land falls away into a valley so that you are actually walking quite high up here, in an area perfumed with something that smells like church incense. Track veers R and eventually descends to the road. 100m before this turn L along track coming from R. After this you can either turn L to road (at bridge) or continue for a short while longer up hill to R on path, joining road further down at a large wayside cross. After that continue down the road to large village of

5km Molinaseca 595m (504/205)
Shops, bars, restaurant. Swimming area in river by bridge.

Enter village passing *Ermita de las Angustias* (R), partly set into the cliffs, and cross the Romanesque *Puente de los Peregrinos* over the River *Meruelo*. Continue along the *Calle Real* (the main street) and when this runs into the main road KSO along it until you reach a tennis court on your R. Turn off road to R and then turn L along a lane // to road. KSO along it as it passes behind the houses on the main road, cross a minor road and KSO slightly uphill along the side of fields. Rejoin road at the top of the hill, just before a crossroads.

After this you can either continue on the main road to Ponferrada, aiming for the tower of the *Basilica de la Encina* or fork L just after the crossroads (the route described here). This option is slightly longer and is not particularly scenic but it does take you onto quieter roads with a great deal less traffic and some parts also have more shade. Fork R at a junction (at a shady square) and at the bottom of the hill KSO (staggered L) through village of

3km Campo (507/202)

KSO at other side and road becomes tarred, passes huge rubbish tip, slaughterhouse and large factory. When this reaches a more minor road turn R along it and KSO, following the road round to the R. Cross the River *Boeza* by the medieval *Puente Mascarón* and immediately afterwards turn L along a road that goes under the railway line. On the other side of this it becomes the *Camino de Bajo San Andrés*. Turn R into the first proper street *(Calle del Hospital)* and at the top (by the church of *San Andrés*), turn up the side of the *Castillo* (on your L) past the Tourist Office.

4km Ponferrada 543m (511/198)

Population 50,000. All facilities, RENFE. Tourist Office.

Large industrial town at the junction of the Rivers Boeza and Sil, taking its name from the iron bridge over the latter. (Today a metal bridge is nothing surprising but was a luxury when it was built, at the end of the twelfth century, and something only possible in an area rich in iron.) The new part of the town is on the west side of the River Sil, the old part on the east, with the thirteenth-century castle built by the Knights Templar, the sixteenth-century Basilica of Nuestra Señora de la Encina (Our Lady of the Evergreen Oak), seventeenth-century town hall and sixteenth-century Torre del Reloj, the only surviving remnant of the former town walls. The tenth-century mozarabic church of Santo Tomás de Ollas is in the suburbs, to the north of the town (and where the camino originally passed).

To leave: from the square near the Basilica go down the steps into the *Calle Ranadero*, turn L to cross bridge *(Avenida de la Puebla)*. Continue to second junction and veer R *(Calle General Gomez Nuñez)* at junction signposted (for vehicles) to "La Coruña". After that KSO (don't fork R again) until you reach a big junction with traffic lights near Ponferrada bus station. Cross over and KSO. This section is not very interesting and you will see an enormous slag heap to the R, then a factory and an electricity sub-station (R). KSO until you reach

3km Columbrianos (514/195)

Bars, shops. (If you find it complicated leaving Ponferrada ask for Columbrianos or the bus station.)

100m before the bridge over the road and just past a petrol station fork L down a minor road (the *Camino Fuentesnuevas*) past factories *(watch out for the yellow arrows again here)*.

200m later this veers L, // to main road. Go under main road and then turn L after 50m along UMUR through fincas. KSO, ignoring turnings to L and R. Cross a minor railway line and continue to the village of

3km Fuentes Nuevas (517/192)
KSO through village *(bar)* and continue to

2km Camponaraya 490m (519/190)
A very long, straggling village with shops, bars, bank.

Turn R onto road and continue through village. [RJ: turn L at house no. 337.] At the end (after 2km) fork L onto a track by a wine cooperative, where the road veers to the R. *From here you can see the mountains of the El Bierzo region all round you and the camino leads through orchards and vines for much of the time.* Turn R at fork. KSO through a small hamlet, turn R at next fork, cross stream and KSO. KSO at next crossing (twice) and KSO to road. Cross and KSO again, ignoring turnings to L and R until you reach the large village of

4km Cacabelos 483m (523/186)
Fountain on R 100m before village. Shops, bars, restaurant, fonda, bank. Swimming area in the river. The last stork on the camino has its "residence" on the church of the Sanctuario de las Angustias on leaving the town.

Continue straight through Cacabelos and out on the other side on the main road. Continue for 2km past hamlet of Pierros and two other unmarked ones. Just past a bridge, 200m after a signpost to "Valtuille" and immediately after a stone house (R) turn R off the road onto a track through fields. Follow path uphill and then down and then turn R at bottom. Turn sharp L onto a track coming from the R. After 100m fork R up hill up track and KSO. [Two tracks join from R.] KSO along green lane until you reach the *Romanesque church of Santiago* (L), by cemetery on the outskirts of Villafranca. *This church has a finely carved Puerta del Perdón, through which pilgrims who were too weak, ill or injured to continue to Santiago entered in order to obtain the same indulgences and remission of their sins as they would have done had they been able to complete their pilgrimage.* Continue downhill into the town.

8km Villafranca del Bierzo 511m (531/178)

Town with all facilities. Tourist Office in Calle Alameda Alta, near church of San Nicolás.

The end of the tenth stage in Aimery Picaud's guide. There are a number of other interesting churches including sixteenth-century Colegiata de Santa María, the Anunciada and the convent church of San Francisco both seventeenth-century) the latter with Baroque cloister. The Castillo-Palacio de los Marqueses dates from the fifteenth century and the Calle del Agua contains some fine old houses, many with armorial devices above the doors.

Between Villafranca and the small Galician village of El Cebreiro at 1300m, 27km away, there are more mountains and a very stiff climb, whether you opt for the high level route or the lower one along the old (and some parts of the new) main road. If you intend to spend the night in El Cebreiro make sure you leave Villafranca early in the day.

To leave: go down the hill from the church of *Santiago* past the *Castillo* (L) and then turn immediately R downhill. Cross street, go down a flight of steps and KSO past a small square and the "Correos" along the *Calle del Agua*. Turn sharp L at the bottom, go up steps and cross the bridge over the River *Burbia*. *After this you chose between the high and the low level route as far as Trabadelo, after which they meet up again:*

a) Continue on the road, flat but busy, though in some parts you use the old sections where it has been straightened out. To do this KSO on the lower (L) of the two waymarked routes and follow the main road, leaving it from time to time as indicated by the yellow arrows.

b) *The high level route is also waymarked, though not always very clearly towards the end. It is much more strenuous but is worth it unless the weather is bad.* Fork R steeply uphill after crossing the bridge and KSO along path which climbs continuously and then passes above woods. Ignore any (of the very few) turnings to L or R. *Splendid views back to Villafranca.*

After a while the track levels out and then starts to descend through chestnut woods. Turn L at junction (walled embankment) and then R at next turn (ignore arrows to L here: both possibilities are waymarked but those to the L fizzle out shortly afterwards) onto minor road, which veers R but then L. After a bend in the road fork R downhill down a FP (watch out for waymarks) which zigzags

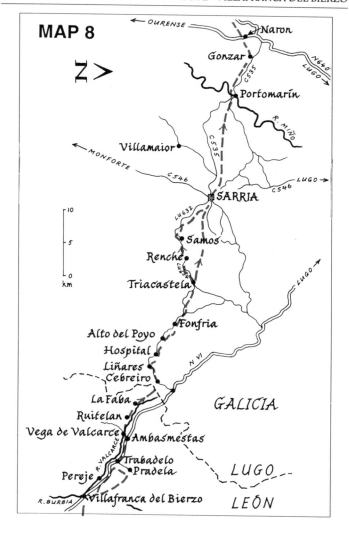

MAP 8

N >

← OURENSE

Naron

Gonzar

N 640

LUGO →

C-535

Portomarín

R. MIÑO

Villamaior

← MONFORTE

C 546

C-535

LUGO →

C 546

SARRIA

LU 633

10

5

0

km

Samos

Renche

LU 677

LUGO →

Triacastela

Fonfria

Alto del Poyo

Hospital

N VI

Liñares

Cebreiro

GALICIA

La Faba

Ruitelan

Vega de Valcarce

Ambasmestas

R. VALCARCE

Trabadelo

Pradela

LUGO

Pereje

R. BURBIA

Villafranca del Bierzo

LEÓN

down (very steeply) to electric pylon. Turn R along road for 20m then fork R off it again down a similar FP, also very steep. Further down path joins road. Turn L and 100m later join road at a concrete structure (water authority building). Turn R along road and continue downhill. [RJ: arrow on tree at this bend - go R uphill.] Join the old main road just above the village of Trabadelo. [RJ: go uphill signposted "Pradela, Sotelo 10".]

10km Trabadelo (541/168)
Bar, panadería, fountain. Bar/restaurant and bar/mesón 100m on other side of main road, just over the river. (Trabadelo is 10km by road from Villafranca, 13-14 by the high level route.)

Continue along the old road for a short distance before joining the main road. Turn R along it and KSO. Cross River *Valcarce* (several times) and then turn R onto a section of the old road. Rejoin main road, pass *hostal/bar* (R) at **Portela** and then fork L onto old road again *(fountain on R, 50m later).*

At a large road junction signposted "Pedrafita 14" veer L down old road though small villages of Ambasmestas *(fountain by Ermita)* and Ambascasas *(you now have the viaduct high above you to the R)* and continue to

6km Vega de Valcarce 630m (547/162)
Shops, bars, farmacía, bank, fonda.

*[The **Castillo de Sarracin** is visible above the village to the L. To visit it - for the view, as it is in ruins - ask if you can leave your rucksack in one of the bars and go up on foot, 20 minutes each way. Start on road and then fork R onto a track leading straight up to it.]*

After Vega de Valcarce the camino starts to climb, gently at first and then steeply, up to El Cebreiro. To begin with it continues to follow the course of the River Valcarce but after that wends its way up through chestnut woods, tiny villages and then into open country where it enters Galicia at 1,200m. Continue on the road to **Ruitelan** *(bar/tabac)* and then to

3km Herrerias 680m (550/159)
Shop on road. The last houses in this village were known as Hospital Inglés, where there was also a chapel where pilgrims who died en route were

buried.

Turn L off road onto a more minor signposted to "La Faba". Veer R over the river and then follow road through village *(bar/shop on L at other end)*. At a "T" junction (signposted to the L to "San Julian 2") KSO(R). At the end of the houses there is a L turn marked "Lindoso 2"; ignore this and KSO(R) here to "La Faba".

Keep R along road and after crossing the second bridge go uphill for 1.5km. Then fork L off the road down a (waymarked) FP and follow its zigzags uphill to the village of

4km La Faba 917m (554/155)
Church, 3 fountains.

Continue through village in a straight line, ignoring turnings to L and R. KSO uphill at end, up shaded lane. Fork R when lane comes out into the open and then KSO to village of

2km Laguna de Castillo 1098m (556/153)
Fountain.

Ignore L turn (downhill). KSO and then L uphill.

Here you will see the first of the Galician marker stones - it is 153km to Santiago from here. These stones, bearing the conch shell motif, are somewhat like old-fashioned milestones, placed at 500 metre intervals along the route from now on (although in fact they fizzle out some 15km before Santiago itself). They are useful not merely to tell you how many more kilometres you still have left before you reach your destination, to reassure you that you aren't lost (particularly as from here onwards the camino frequently picks its way through a veritable maze of old lanes and tracks, with constant changes of direction) but also to tell you the names of the places you are in, as many of the villages you will go through after this are far too small to have name boards. Galicia is riddled with green lanes, none of which ever have signposts, so that these marker stones, redundant though they might initially appear, are in fact very useful. In the province of La Coruña they are also used as waymarks and have arrows on them to indicate changes of direction, whether or not they coincide with the usual 0.5km sitings.

Unlike Navarre and Castille-León, where the villages are bigger but very widely spaced apart, those in Galicia are often extremely small but very close to one another and you are not usually far from a building of some

sort.

After 1km you will enter Galicia, in the province of Lugo (*large marker stone to L of camino*). Then, after a further 1km, past a walled-in wood (R) and a large stone barn (R) you will emerge onto the road at

2km El Cebreiro 1,300m (558/151)
Hostal (meals and accommodation), fountain.

National Monument. A tiny village consisting partly of "pallozas", round thatched dwellings of Celtic origin, one of which is now a small museum. The village originated with the pilgrim route and the Hostal San Giraldo was originally a hospital, from the eleventh century to 1854, founded by monks from the French abbey of Saint Gérard d'Aurillac. The church of Santa María contains relics and a twelfth-century statue of the Virgin which reputedly inclined its head after a miracle that took place in the sixteenth century.

Magnificent views all round in good weather. At night, if it is clear, the Milky Way (used by pilgrims in centuries gone by to guide them as they walked ever due west) is easily seen as there are no street or other lights anywhere in sight - a rare chance to see all the stars against a completely black sky.

Leave on road and KSO to hamlet of

3km Liñares (561/148)
Bar/tabac, fountain on L.

Fork L off road, enter village, pass church and rejoin road 1km further on at

1km Alto de San Roque 1264m (562/147)
Chapel of San Roque, panoramic views.

Turn R off road onto grassy track. Rejoin it again at K146. At K145.5 enter **Hospital da Condesa** (*church*). Fork R in village off road. KSO *Fountain*. At end of village continue on lane and rejoin road just before K145. Continue on road for another 400m then fork R to minor road (signposted to "Sabugos Busnullan"). Turn L up lane 200m further on, up hill (small hut on R of road). Fork L at junction, join track coming from L and KSO. Pass through **Padornelo** (K143, 1275m). Emerge onto minor road at church - KSO for 22m and when road bends R KSO up track that climbs very steeply to

4.5km Alto del Poyo 1,337m (566.5/142.5)
Small group of houses with bar/shop, mesón.

Capilla Santa María. From here to Triacastela (13km) the route is downhill all the way. After that, and in Galicia in general, the camino is often shaded so it is cool and pleasant to walk in, even in the middle of the day, with speckled sunlight. It is, however, often wet and/or misty in this part, especially in the mornings.

Continue on road for 2km, leaving it shortly before K140.5 and continue on green lane, shortcutting road as far as

3.5km Fonfría del Camino 1290m (570/139)
There was a pilgrim refuge here as early as 1535 and which continued to function until the middle of the last century. It offered free "light, salt, water and two blankets" to the able-bodied, "bread, an egg and lard" to the sick. The village takes its name from its "cool fountain".

KSO through village, fork L at end and KSO (road to L). Return to road briefly at K137.5 and turn R off road to lane. 200m further on cross road and fork L off road onto track. Continue to road but do not join it: continue L instead, to village of **Viduedo** (K136.5, *Ermita de San Pedro on R*) and veer L through it. *Panoramic views in all of this section, down to Triacastela, on a clear day. [R]: 135.5 to 136.5 fairly level.]*

Ignore R turn before K136. Pass K135.5 at **Monte Calderon**. At junction after K135 turn R downhill, turn R at bottom at barn then L at village of **Filloval** (K133.5). After 100m cross road and turn hard R downhill down lane. KSO(L) at fork and continue gently down a grassy lane. [Track joins from back R.] KSO to road. Cross road and continue downhill (R) on other side. [Track joins from back L.] KSO.

Enter village of **As Pasantes** (K132) and fork L downhill. Fork L at Ermita and continue down shaded green lanes. [Track joins from back R.] KSO to **Ramil** (130.5). Fork R in village and KSO downhill to

9km Triacastela 665m (579/130)
Shop, bars, restaurant, fonda, bank.

End of the eleventh stage in Aimery Picaud's guide. Church of Santiago.

95

Continue down the main street and at the end you can chose between two routes to Sarria: a) turn L, via Samos, on the road all the way or b) turn R, via San Xil, along green lanes, paths and a few minor roads. This is much more pleasant as a walk but it is also more strenuous and there are no shops or bars and only one fountain along the way. Which route you chose will probably depend on the weather (the San Xil option can be very muddy if it has been raining) and whether or not you want to visit the monastery at Samos or stay in the village.

A. Route via Samos

Turn L in Triacastela, pass modern pilgrim statue at edge of road *(fountain to L by market hall)*, cross the bridge over the River *Ouribio* (which you will cross and recross several more times before Sarria) and continue on main road. *This winds in and out and climbs up and down and is best covered on a Sunday when there are no lorries and, hopefully, not too many cars either. This route is not waymarked but is very easy to follow. According to the signpost Samos is 11km from Triacastela but it is probably only 8 or 9. The road is often shaded, at least in part.* It passes through the hamlets of **Real** and **Renche** *(small bar/shop)* and by or above several others before going downhill into

8km Samos 532m
Shop, bars, restaurant, hostal.

Small village dominated by a very large Benedictine monastery (National Monument - guided tours available); this formerly housed some 500 monks but today there are only a handful left.

KSO on the main road for Sarria (12km). *2km after Samos there is a new hotel/restaurant on the L.* The road continues to wind up and down as before and there appear to be no short cuts for the bends. When you reach Sarria watch out for a turning L off the main road (just before two huge blocks of flats) with a "señal" *(pilgrim with hat and stick on blue and white background)*. This is where you join up with the other route coming from San Xil [from a turning to your R off the main road]. Follow the road round to the L and then R past K112 (Sarria) and continue as below.

B. Route via San Xil
Turn R in Triacastela, along a minor road. Fork R at fork along

The Cathedral and Bishop's Palace at Astorga
The castle of the Templars and the River Sil at Ponferrada

Descending to the village of El Acebo
The route between Villafranca del Bierzo and O Cebreiro

Samos. Monastery

UMUR, turn L at next fork and go through hamlet of **Balsa**. KSO. Veer L at end, cross bridge and then turn R uphill past farm and Ermita (K127.5).

Emerge onto road 200m before K126.5 (**San Xil** - *a small hamlet with only a few houses*). Turn R and continue on road (fountain on R, 200m later) for 1km. At K124.5 (**Alto de Riocabo**, 896m, *good views on a clear day*) turn R up road with shale surface, cross track after 10m and KSO along another one, downhill to K124 (**A Focara**).

At K123.5 KSO(R) (ie. ignore L turn). KSO. [Track joins from back R.] KSO, passing K123 at **O Real**. KSO downhill to L of field (R). KSO at crossing, down walled lane (rock walls). Pass K122.5 at **Montan**. KSO at junction to L, enter village and turn R along lane.

Church tower, Hospital de Condesa

KSO(L) at next fork.

Shortly after K122 join bigger track coming from R. KSO, ignoring turns to L and R. Pass K121.5 at **Fontearanda**. KSO. Join road shortly before K121 at **Zoo Mondaveiga** and turn R along it. Then turn hard L down track leading "backwards" off road into woods - be careful not to miss this turning (and therefore continue along road, downhill, to a group of houses) as it is not at all obvious. [RJ: turn L up track uphill shortly before passing K121.]

Turn hard R at bottom of hill along track which then veers round to L. Veer R at fork. [Track joins from back R, slightly uphill.] Join road at K120, turn L. Pass K199.5 at **Furela**. KSO on road, fork R up track. Pass K118.5 at Pinton (*bar?*), fork L down lane to village and then turn R. KSO at junction at end of village.

Continue on road and fork L down a lane at K117.5 (**Calvor**). Join road again at bottom, turn R and follow road round. Pass K116.5 at **Aquiada**. Enter hamlet of **Hospital** (K116, *so-named because it once had a pilgrim hospice and church*) and KSO along minor road to Sarria, passing **San Marmede** (K115), **San Pedro** (K114.5), **Carballal** (K114), **Vigo de Sarria** (K113) until you enter the town itself at K112.

Cross over the road from Samos. KSO and follow road round to

R. Cross bridge over the River *Ouribio*. KSO along the Rua de Peregrino and then turn R and immediately L up a steep street with steps (the *Escalinata Maior*). Continue uphill almost straight ahead, up the *Rúa Maior*. At the top (before you get to the Castillo and *fountain*) turn R past the old prison along the *Avenida de la Feria*. KSO past K111 (R) and the market (L) and turn L by the cemetery and go downhill.

18km Sarria 420m (597/112)
All facilities.

The old part of the town is up on the hill and includes a church dedicated to the Galician martyr Santa Marina, the Romanesque church of El Salvador, the Convento de la Magdalena, the remains of the medieval castillo at the top of the hill and several old houses with armorial devices over the doors.

The section from Sarria to Portomarín is one of the most quiet and peaceful of the camino but before you leave Sarria make sure you have enough food (and water) as apart from one bar off the path at Mercado da Sera there are no shops, no other bars and nowhere at all at get anything to eat or drink until you reach Portomarín. The route passes through many villages but they are all extremely small, with no facilities of any kind.

Turn R at the bottom of the hill by the cemetery and then turn L over the medieval *Ponte Aspera* (K110.5) down a lane to the Madrid-La Coruña railway line. The path continues alongside the track before bending L and then R to become a green lane. Cross railway line (carefully!) at K109.5 (**Sancti Michaelis**) and then turn L down a lane // to the railway line. Cross stream by footbridge and turn R up hill. At fork turn L up hill *(huge trees)*. At the top the path bends L. KSO through fields, pass walled orchard on your L and turn R along track. KSO.

Pass **As Paredes** at K109. [RJ: fork R at K108.5.] Turn L onto minor road and village of **Vilei** (K108). Follow road through village and KSO at road. *Good views to L.* Road bends to R just before church at

5km Barbedelo 580m (602/107)
Romanesque church of Santiago, a National Monument and worth a visit for its frescoes.

To continue either KSO past a large white building (R) or go to R of building (ie. it is on your L) and go through village, joining road again at end and turning R along it.

At the top of the hill turn L off the road into a lane at K106.5 (**Rente**). Enter hamlet from R and at end join road and turn L along it (*grove of oak trees on L is a good spot for a rest*). Pass K106 at **Mercado da Sera**. KSO. Cross another road and KSO. (*Bar signposted a few metres off to L.*) Veer R behind farm and continue down tree-lined lane. Cross farm road and KSO. At end (K105) turn L down a wide lane. [RJ: turn R here.]

KSO, passing K104.5 at **Marzan O Real** and at crossing (wall in front and electricity tower) turn R (this is hard to find). Turn L at K104. Cross road and KSO on minor road. Pass K103.5 at **Leiman**. Turn L at fork and continue on road (K103 Peruscallo) to village of **Peruscallo** itself (K102.5). *Fountain to R off camino.* Fork L at end and follow lane round to R.

Here you encounter one of the many "horreos" typical of this region - long narrow rectangular stone or brick storehouses raised up on stilts and used for potatoes, corncobs etc. They have a cross on top of the roof at one end and a decorative knob at the other and vary enormously in size; some are only 2 or 3 metres long but others may be as long as 15 to 20.

Turn L 100m further on into lane and then R at K102 (**Cortiñas**). KSO through fields and enter hamlet of **Lavandeira**. Continue and join minor road at curve in village. Continue and fork R. KSO on road and then fork L off road to lane. At crossing at K101.5 (**Casal**) KSO down walled lane. 100m further on turn R at crossing with minor road and then turn L down lane. At end KSO on road. [RJ: KSO to lane at bend in road.]

KSO down lane to K100 (**Brea**). KSO at fork (to L) and KSO at fork (to L again). Go uphill to road. [RJ: continue past turn to L at farm and take the next turning on the L, which gives directly onto the road.]

Turn R and KSO through village of **Brea**. KSO to vill..ge of **Morgade** (K99.5, *fountain*). KSO then fork L downhill outside village. After K99 emerge at top of hill. Track levels out - good views. KSO. Turn R at next fork to village of **Ferreiros**. To enter village (*fountain*) turn L, otherwise pass above to R of it. At road take R fork (you arrive at the bottom of a "U"). Turn L at end of village down minor

Galician wayside cross

road *(tower of cemetery chapel visible 50m below you at K98 (**Mirallos**, Romanesque church of Santa María)*.

Fork L at top of hill to village of **Pena** (K97.5). Fork R uphill then fork L onto road coming from your R and continue along it. Pass villages of **Couto** and then **Rozas** *(fountain)*. At K69.5 turn R off road to shady lane and turn R at next fork.

Pass K96 (**Pena dos Corros**) and then K95.5 (**Moimentos**). Cross track and KSO downhill to minor road. Cross it and continue straight on down lane veering L. At next road turn R along it and after 100m, at large wayside crucifix and K95 (**Cotarelo Mercadoiro**) turn L down lane off road.

KSO at junction (to L). Enter village of **Moutrás** (K94.5) and continue out of it in a straight line. [RJ: turn R.] Join road coming from R and KSO. After K94 it is downhill all the way down to Portomarín (4km). Turn L at K93.5, turn L and then immediately R down a track *(view of Portomarín ahead).*

KSO to road. [RJ: fork L uphill and take L of two tracks.]

Turn L into minor road [RJ: fork R into village], pass K93 (**Parrocha**) and then veer L through village and KSO along road with pinewoods on either side. At end (K92.5) turn R down lane. [After 500m another track joins from back R.] Track bends R. [RJ: take upper track ahead, uphill.]

Pass K92 (**Vilachá**), cross road and KSO for 50m, turn R into village (K91.5). *Dogs!* Veer L along main street, veer L, then R and fork R at end. KSO on road. At road junction at K91 veer R (contrary to what you might expect) and follow road round to your L and then downhill (bar on R). Turn L uphill at bottom at K90. In front of you you will see the River *Miño* and the Embalse de Belezar (reservoir). Cross bridge over the river, go up steep flight of steps ahead and enter

17km Portomarín 550m (619/90)
Shops, bars, restaurant, hostal, youth hostel.

The original town was flooded when the River Miño was dammed up to build the reservoir in the early 1960s and the new town built up on the hill above it. Before this took place, however, the fortified Romanesque church of San Nicolás was taken to pieces stone by stone (the numbers can still be seen today) and rebuilt on its present town centre site. The portal is by Master Mateo (who built the Portico de la Gloria in the Cathedral in Santiago). The other church in Portomarín, San Pedro, is also Romanesque.

There are 7km of road walking in this next stretch but there is not usually too much traffic. To leave Portomarín: go down the main street away from the church (the dam and river are to your L), cross river by footbridge and turn R on other side up minor road. Turn L further on up track at K89. Continue up hill for 1km *(factory at top, on L)*, when track levels out. Good views. Pass K87.5 at **Cortapezas**.

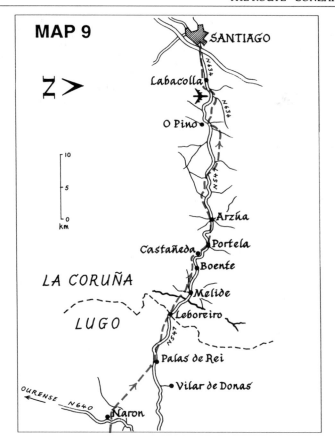

When you reach the road, just before K87, KSO along it. Pass K85.5 (**Toxibó**), K82.5 (**Gonzar**) and enter

8km Gonzar (627/82)
Small village with Romanesque church of Santa María.
    200m after K81.5, at **Castromaior** turn L onto minor road.

Galician marker stone

Follow road through village, veering L and KSO uphill on road. At junction with another road (K80) turn L. 200m after K79 turn L off road onto track. Pass K78.5 at **Hospital de la Cruz** (*site of former pilgrim hospice*). Continue through village, fork L uphill at end and continue to main road (K78). Cross it and KSO on minor road

4.5km Ventas de Narón (631.5/77.5)
Small hamlet with unmarked bar (the first of many you will meet in remote places) at crossroads to R (it also has rooms). [RJ: fork L after crossing road.]

Enter village and continue through it (K77), continuing to climb until you pass K76.5, **Sierra de Ligonde** at 765m (*panoramic views on a clear day*), after which the route leads you downhill. *Shortly after K75 (**Previsa**) there is an interesting wayside crucifix to L of road, by an enormous tree (good place for a rest).* Continue through village of **Ligonde** (K73.5, *site of a pilgrim hospice in former times*) to

4.5km Eirexe (636/73)
Bar.

The village takes its name from the Gallego word for "church" (and this one has a Romanesque portal with sculpture of Daniel and animals on south wall).

Turn L to leave village (*fountain at top of hill on L after 200m*). KSO to K72 (**As Cruces**) at crossroads. Cross over and KSO downhill along minor road, passing K71 (**Portos Vilar de Donas**).

*[From here a detour of 3km (each way) is recommended, along a lane to R, to **Vilar de Donas** with its Romanesque church of El Salvador, a National Monument, with fourteenth-century wall paintings and effigies of the Knights of the Order of Santiago who took it over in 1184.]*

After **Portos** stay on this road until just after K70 (**Lestedo**). Follow road uphill through village. 200m after K70 turn R off road down lane. [Track joins from L.] KSO. [RJ: fork L.]

If you miss this turning continue uphill instead and you will enter the village of **Valos** at K69.5; turn R here along a road which then veers R and brings you out on the main road. Turn L along it and KSO to KM31 (road numbering system).

KSO, ignoring turns to L and R. Go down lane. cross stream, KSO uphill to road. Turn L along it. KSO to road at KM31 and turn

L and then R onto road. Pass K68 (**Ave Nostre/Lamelas**). Cross minor road and KSO, ignoring turns to L and R. Pass K67.5 (**Alto de Rosario**). After 200m return to road and KSO. At K67 (**O Rosario**) turn L off road to UMUR, turn R through village and KSO. Pass sports centre (on your L) with swimming pool, continue straight on downhill, veering R, pass church and enter

7km Palas de Rei 565m (643/66)
Small town with all facilities but no very interesting features.

End of the twelfth stage in Aimery Picaud's guide and the start of the thirteenth, the last, to Santiago.

To leave: cross main street and continue downhill on other side, veer R (*fountain*) and continue on main road (N547) to **Caraballal** (K64). At K63.5 (where the main road starts to turn R at the top of the hill) leave the road and turn L down a FP (waymarked). [Track joins from back R.] KSO, pass K63 at **A Lagua**, continue down to road (coming from back L) and turn R along it for 20m and then KSO(L) down a lane when road bends to L. Continue downhill at K62.5 (**San Julian do Camino**, *fountain*) to another road. Turn L and continue through village past church (*several horreos*). Pass K62 at **Pallota**.

Continue on road. When it bends L KSO down a lane. At the bottom KSO (L) along another road and cross a bridge over the River *Pambre*. Turn R after 50m up a lane (K61). [RJ: fork L downhill midway.] Ignore L turn and KSO. Turn L onto road at the end just before K60 (**Casanova**). KSO(R) at top of hill and then turn L down lane (K59.5). Turn R downhill at fork.

Cross road at bottom (K58.5 **Porto de Bois**) and KSO along track through a field. Cross bridge over the River *Porto de Bois* and KSO uphill. Pass K58 at **Campanilla** and KSO. [Track joins from back L.] Turn R along road, pass K57.5 at **Cato** and 200m further on enter the province of La Coruña.

Here the milestones, normally on your R, are not only at 500m intervals but are also used, with appropriate arrows on them, to indicate changes of direction. [RJ: they will therefore be on your L - facing away from you.]

Continue for a short distance to the main road (N547), signposted "Santiago 60, Melide 6". Turn L at junction (*bar/shop on L*).

Turn L off main road after 100m along a track (Melide now

visible ahead) leading to village of

9.5km Leboreiro (652.5/56.5)
Fountain. Simple Romanesque church of Santa María (the building opposite was the former pilgrim hospital), rollo.

KSO, enter walled lane and then cross reconstructed copy of old bridge over the River *Seco*. Turn R at junction (*fountain*) at K56 (**Disicabo**). KSO. Turn L shortly before a large concrete barn, pass K55.5 (**Magdalena**). KSO and then turn L at K55 along tree-lined track // to main road for 1.5km

Continue down a lane, join UMUR coming from back R (K53). KSO for 300m and then fork L downhill. Join road at K52.5, turn L and 100m later cross bridge over the River Furelos in the village of **Furelos** itself. Turn L ahead, pass church and turn L again through village. KSO and then fork R at K52. Continue uphill for 200m, join road coming from R and KSO for 100m. Cross a road, go up a UMUR for 300m, fork R (K51 **Melide**) and 20m later enter main street [by cycle/moto shop for RJ].

5.5km Melide 454m (658/51)
All facilities.

Pleasant small town with public garden in centre, several "pulperías" (stalls or restaurants serving squid). Churches of San Pedro, Sancti Spiritu (former monastery church, with pilgrim hospital opposite) and, up on the hill as you leave the town, the Romanesque church of Santa María.

Continue along main street past public garden (L) and turn R at large ornate *fountain* at junction and then turn L along the *Rúa San Pedro* and its continuation the *Rúa Principal*. (Another fountain in small square to R.) Pass church of *Santa María* (L) and cemetery (L), both at the top of the hill, and KSO downhill along lane to road at the bottom. Cross it and enter hamlet of **Santa María** (*shop, bar*). [RJ: cross road and go up lane veering R.]

Turn R 200m further on down minor road, past a chapel and another cemetery, passing the first of the many eucalyptus trees you will encounter from now on. *From here too, until the outskirts of Santiago, the route leads in and out of the woods most of the time so that although the temperature may be quite high in summer walking is still very pleasant as much of the route is shaded.*

Pass lavadero and *fountain* (R), pass K49.5 (**Carballal**). KSO for 1km and enter woods (*pine and eucalyptus*). Cross River *Raído* and KSO. Turn L at junction and continue gently uphill all the time. When you come out of the woods KSO. Turn R onto a UMUR leading to the road at K47.5 (**Raído**). Turn L along road for 100m then turn L again down a track. KSO at road. Pass K46.8 at **Parabispo**. When road bends sharply to L KSO(R) down a shady track. KSO [track enters from back R].

At **Peroxa** (K45.5) cross a lane and KSO. After 50m turn L down another road and then R in village (*fountain*). Join road and turn L at

6km Boente (664/45)
Bar on road.
Fountain at crossing, rollo, church of Santiago.

Turn R at church and then L straight away and KSO down UMUR to road (K44.5), cross it and continue downhill towards the River *Boente*, keeping straight on (L) at fork. Go under road, KSO uphill, veer R and then L, climbing steeply up again to main road. Turn L along it, pass K43 (**Castañeda**) and KSO. After 300m turn L to minor road signposted to "Rio Pomar Doroña". KSO (R) when road bends to L. Pass K42.5 (**Pedrido**). KSO(R) at junction (to L) and turn L at next junction (K42 **Río**), continuing uphill all the time. *This section is less complicated than it sounds as, in effect, you are going in a straight line, although up- and downhill a lot, shortcutting the hairpins in the road.*

KSO at next crossing (// to main road) and continue uphill again (steep). At the top turn R uphill (again!) and then veer R and then L. 10m after K40.5 the camino crosses a new road in a very steep cutting, by means of a footbridge. KSO through woods. Cross another road, turning R and then immediately L (dangerous crossing). KSO downhill, crossing the bridge over the River *Iso* at the bottom in the village of

5km Ribadiso de Baixo (669/40)
The first house on the R by the river, a pilgrim hospice in medieval times, is being restored as a refuge.

Continue uphill (ignore L turn), pass K39.5 (**Ribadiso**) and continue uphill again. Turn L uphill (yet again!) at junction and R (uphill) onto main road. [RJ: turn L down road signposted to "Rendal".] Continue on road to

2.5km Arzua 389m (671.5/37.5)
Small town with all facilities.

Churches of Santa María (parish church) and La Magdalena (former Augustinian convent with a pilgrim hospital).

On entering the town fork L to the *Rúa Cima de Luga*, // to main road and KSO. Pass church of *Santa María* (R), go down *Rúa do Carmen*, cross another street and KSO. Fork L (K36.5) just before a factory, down a lane and KSO.

Pass K36 (**As Barrosas**), cross track and KSO. Pass *Capilla San Lazaro* (L). Turn R 50m later along farm road to main road. Turn L along this for 200m then fork L down track (at bend in road). This is // to the road at first but then leads back to the road again at a farm just after K35. Turn L on road for 300m then turn R to minor road signposted to "Fontavila Cortobe" and "Pazos Sevio".

Turn L 200m later onto another minor road leading to village of **Fondavilla** (K34) and then **Cotorbe** (K33.8). Fork L to leave village then R to next village of **Pereiriña** and fork L at K33.5. Continue downhill, cross stream and then fork R (at K33) uphill to minor road (K32.5). Cross it and LSO till you join another track coming from R at **Tabernavella** (K32). Turn R along it and then KSO (R) when it bends to L.

KSO at junction (K31.5) and KSO past village of **Calzada** (K31.5). Cross minor road and KSO. KSO (L) at junction to R. Ignore next L turn and KSO. KSO at next junction, then cross minor road and KSO, ignoring turns to L and R until you reach houses at bend in minor road. KSO down lane to L of building and at *fountain* and minor road junction (K29.2 **Calle**) turn R and then immediately L down lane under horreo.

After 50m turn R (ie. KSO) onto minor road for 20m then turn L along road. Turn R down lane past lavadero; cross minor road and fork R down lane which then veers L. At bend in minor road fork R along another lane, which then veers L. KSO, ignoring turns to L and R till you reach a minor road with roadside crucifix. (*Café/bar 200m to L.*) Cross road, continue on another straight ahead for 100m,

109

then fork L at K28 to track. Pass clusters of houses at **Boavista** (K27.8).

(The main road is // for much of this section so, once again, it is not as complicated as it may seem.) At next minor road <u>do not KSO</u> but turn L and then immediately R under trees. Turn L along minor road and then at crossing a few metres further on KSO along lane. L at fork shortly afterwards and KSO, ignoring turnings. (The main road is // to you here to the L.) Pass K26.3 **Salceda**. KSO (track becomes a minor road here). Cross a minor road.

12km Salceda (683.5/25.5)
KSO through village and fork L to lane. At end, join main road and turn R along it. *Bar/shop at 100m on R.*
[RJ: turn L down lane after last house on L after bar.]
100m after bar fork R onto lane at side of house (waymarked). Cross a minor road. KSO to main road, cross this and after 50m fork L down a lane and continue uphill past K24.5 at **Xen**. Cross a minor road and KSO. *(Bar 30m to R on main road.)*
At K24 **Bas** (junction to L) KSO. Emerge on minor road and KSO. [RJ: fork L to lane.] When you reach the main road cross it and KSO on other side (lane). KSO(L) at junction (to R).
Pass K23.5 (**Brea**). Turn L at minor road and then almost immediately turn R down lane. KSO to a farm (K23 **Rabina**) and turn L (farm on R). Turn L at junction and then R onto main road. Continue along this for 1km and at **Empalme** at top of hill turn R to minor road *(bar/café, shop, restaurant)*. Turn L 100m later along side of woods (K21.5) Enter eucalyptus woods (// to main road). Go downhill out of woods, cross main road (K21) and KSO down track to the chapel of

5km Santa Irene (688.5/20.5)
Bar
Continue to main road, go along it for 50m and cross it (carefully) at bend (very dangerous crossing - try to cross it either above or below bend). Go down lane till you reach the road again. Cross it and fork L down a track and fork R (K19.5) to woods.
At minor road (join it at bend - bar 100m to R on main road) KSO (**Rua** K19). Ignore turns and KSO to main road again. Cross it and

KSO on other side up lane to eucalyptus woods. Ignore turns to L and R and KSO through woods till you come out at the side of a very large hangar/warehouse (on the R). Turn R in front of it along tarmac road and past college sports ground. Pass K17.5 (**Pedrouzo**) at the end.

3.5km Arca (692/17)
Shop and 3 bars.

To enter the village turn L after stadium. To continue on the camino turn R and then L (after *bar* on L) into woods again.

Turn L at the end onto a minor road (K16.9 **San Anton**). Follow road round to R, turn L and KSO (ignore next turn to L) on road which then becomes a track. Turn L to enter woods at K16.5. After 100m fork L at fork in woods. R at next fork.

At the end of the woods turn L and then immediately R along track that goes along the side of the woods (R) and then veers L to join a minor road. Turn R along it and pass **Amenal** (K15), and turn R at junction. Then turn L and continue to main road.

2km Amenal (694/15)
Bar/tabac. Small supermarket 200m further on on (L) main road.

Cross road and KSO up shady lane. Cross a minor road and KSO. Cross a track and fork L into woods. *Here the camino originally led straight on but now you have to do a detour to go round the edge of Santiago airport.* Turn R at K12.5 and continue to main road.

Turn L along it at K12 for 500m, then cross it, follow footpath along RH side of road and then turn R into the small hamlet of **San Paio**. Turn L at church and then take middle (minor) road up steep hill. At the top, at a "T" junction, take the middle path straight on. After 100m cross road and KSO. At junction with similar track 500m further on turn L and KSO, following lane which then becomes a minor road, into the village of

5km Labacolla (699/10)
Hostal, bars, shop. The only fountain is 100m up lane off main road (to L) opposite bar San Miguel (after chapel), down some steps to L of lane.

Small village where, traditionally, pilgrims washed in the river and generally made themselves presentable before entering Santiago. If it is

already fairly late in the day when you arrive in Labacolla consider staying here so that you can complete the final stage in a leisurely way the following morning.

The original camino went past the Capilla San Roque, on what is now the main road. To continue you can either follow this and then turn L when you see the TV masts and TV station up road (L) to Monte de Gozo or turn L to main road below church (temporarily away from Santiago), go along it for 100m and then cross it and turn R along minor road signposted to "Vilamaior". This takes you along quiet roads more or less // to the main road.

Follow road round to R and KSO to village of **Vilamaior** (2km: *there are no longer any marker posts).* Turn L in village and then R. KSO. When you get to a junction (after 2km) with a campsite to your L turn L past TV station (TVE Galicia).

4km Monte del Gozo 368m (703/6)
Campsite.

To visit the Monte del Gozo (Monxoi in gallego) continue for 50m. *This was the place from where pilgrims could see the Cathedral of Santiago for the first time after their long journey and was thus known as "Mount Joy". It was formerly a quiet green hill but after the Pope's visit to Santiago in 1989 it was levelled to make room for the vast crowds and there is now a large complex of accommodation, amphitheatre, car parks and restaurants being built.*

To continue to Santiago turn R (or L if you have come from the Monte del Gozo) down minor road by TV station. Turn R after 500m (at bottom of hill) and then immediately L along a minor road leading to the hamlet of **San Marco** (don't go as far as the main road). *At the top of the next hill you come to the Capilla San Marco which has, in fact, a much better view of Santiago than you get from the Monte del Gozo. Surrounded by trees it is a good place for a final rest.*

Continue on past chapel, downhill. When you get to the bottom, just before the main road and just past a house (L) with two stone rollos in its garden and a lot of very large concrete animals (dinosaurs etc.) go down a flight of steps to L and cross bridge over motorway. *(Like many cities, the outskirts of Santiago are not very inviting.)*

The 13th century former monastery church of San Salvador at Vilar de Donas

En route from O Cebreiro to Triacastella
Santiage de Compostela from the park of Santa Susana

4km San Lazaro (707/2)

Suburb of Santiago.

After crossing the motorway KSO along the *Rúa do Valiño* (ie. the road you are already on) passing the church of *San Lazaro*. Fork L off the main road down the *Barrio das Fontiñas* when you see a very large modern housing complex to the L below the road. When you reach a big junction with traffic lights (*the Avenida de Lugo L goes to the new town*) continue uphill along the *Calle Fuente de los Concheiros*.

After passing a small square (L) with the cross of the *Homo Sancto* the road becomes the *Rúa San Pedro*. Follow this down to the *Porto do Camino*, the traditional pilgrim entry point, then go up the *Rúa des Casas Reias*, cross the *Plaza de Parga*, the *Plaza de Animas*, turn L into the *Plaza Cervantes* and then R down the *Calle Azabachería* to the Cathedral. Go round to the front, in the huge *Plaza de Obradoiro*, and enter the Cathedral by the Portico de la Gloria.

2km Santiago de Compostela 264m (709/0)

Population 80,000. All facilities. RENFE. Accommodation in all price ranges. Two campsites: one on the main road to La Coruña, the other at As Cancelas (on outskirts). Tourist Office: 43 Rúa do Vilar (near Cathedral).

The most important of the many places of interest in Santiago (all in the old town) is the Cathedral, part Romanesque, part Baroque, with its magnificent Portico de la Gloria and façade giving onto the Plaza del Obradoiro. The Cathedral also houses what is probably the world's biggest censer (incense burner), the famous "Botafumeiro". It is made of silver and weighs nearly 80 kilos, requiring a team of eight men and a system of pulleys to set it in motion, swinging, at ceiling level from one end of the transept to the other. Guide books (in English) are available from the bookshops in the Rúa do Villar (near the Cathedral) or in the new town (eg. Follas Novas, 1 Calle Nueva). Try to spend two or three days in Santiago, as there is much to see and do.

If you have time two pilgrim destinations outside the city are worth visiting. <u>Padrón</u> is the place where the boat bringing Saint James to Galicia in AD44 is believed to have arrived and also contains the museum of Rosalía de Castro, the nineteenth-century Galician poet; it can be reached easily by train (some 20kms from Santiago railway station). <u>Finisterre</u>, the end of the known world in former times and the end of the route for many pilgrims in centuries gone by, can be reached by bus (95kms) from Santiago bus station, everyday except Sunday. If you prefer, however, you can continue there on foot, a three day journey described in Appendix B.

Santiago de Compostela

Appendices

APPENDIX A - SAINT JEAN PIED-DE-PORT TO RONCESVALLES (see map p30)

Saint Jean-Pied-de-Port ("Saint John at the foot of the pass") **180m.** *Population 1,800. All facilities. Gîte d'étape, campsite, Syndicat d'Initiative, SNCF.*

Small border town on the River Nive, capital of the Basque province of Basse Navarre. Several places of interest: Citadelle, overlooking the town, with its system of ramparts (being restored); access either from the top end of the Rue de la Citadelle or by staircase ("escalier de la poterne") leading up from the footpath along the river by the side of the church - worth the climb on a clear day. Prison des Evêques. Musée de la Pelote. Eglise Notre-Dame-du-bout-du-pont. Pont Romain. The different "portes" (Saint Jacques, d'Espagne, for example). Note architecture of Basque-style houses with often ornate wooden overhangs at roof level, balconies. If you have time to spare the SI has a booklet of waymarked walks in the area.

Traditionally pilgrims entered the town by the Porte Saint Jacques at the top of the Rue de la Citadelle and those who have followed the GR65 will have done the same. After that there are two routes to Roncesvalles, one via *Valcarlos*, the other by the *Route Napoléon*. The former is a little shorter (22km) and not so steep but is on the road nearly all the way. However, if the weather is very bad or visibility poor, you may prefer to take this.

If so, from the *Rue de la Citadelle* go through the *Porte d'Espagne* (passing the church on your L, *fountain*), cross the bridge over the River *Nive*, go up the *Rue d'Espagne* but then turn R into the *Rue d'Uhart*. Continue along *Place Floquet* (under the jardin public), through the rampart gateway and then, after 20m, bear L when you see a signpost to "Arnéguy 8. Frontière d'Espagne". Follow the road up to the border at Arnéguy on the French side, cross it and enter

8km Valcarlos 365m

Border town on the Spanish side, with shops, tourist office and bank (not

always open).

Church of Santiago contains a life-size representation of Santiago Matamoros.

Continue along the road as it climbs up and up. Between Arneguy and Ibañeta you will see yellow arrows and also the red "balises" of the French waymarking system leading you off the route at intervals, to short-cut some of the many bends, but these are not at all easy to follow once you are off the road, in <u>very</u> dense forest. Follow the road up and then, when it reaches the top, continue downhill to the

10km Puerto d'Ibañeta 1057m

Continue as described on page 119.

*The **Route Napoléon** leads over the Pyrenees via the Col de Bentarte and the Porte de Cize. It is 27km long and is a spectacular route on a clear day. It was also the one favoured by pilgrims in centuries gone by because, although it was much more strenuous, it was also exposed for most of the way, and they were thus less likely to be ambushed by bandits than on the densely wooded route through Valcarlos. It follows the path of the old Roman road from Bordeaux to Astorga and is normally accessible without any trouble (ie. too much snow) from May to October. If you are a fairly fit walker allow at least seven hours actual walking (excluding stops); if not, allow much longer, especially if it is very windy (when it will always be against you). Start early in the day (eg. 6.30am in summer or as soon as it is light) not only to avoid the heat but also being high up later in the day when the light is going and you are tired. Take <u>enough food and water</u> with you, including the following morning's breakfast.*

Go down the *Rue de la Citadelle*, past the church of *Notre-Dame-du-bout-du-pont* ("Our Lady at the end of the bridge", *fountain*), through the *Porte d'Espagne*, cross the bridge over the River *Nive* and continue on up the *Rue d'Espagne*, following the red and white "balises" of the GR65. KSO, continue up the *Route Saint Michel* for approx. 100m, bear L at a fork and after 20m you will come to a junction with the *Route Maréchal Harrispe*. Take this (ie. bear R off the *Route Saint Michel*, which bends round to the L). *There is a sign here, with red and white balises, saying "Chemin de Saint Jacques de Compostelle. Route des Portes de Cize. Summus Pyrenaeus de la Voie Romana."* (*Fountain on L.*) KSO and after approx. 500m there is a small junction and the road name changes to *"Route Napoléon"*.

Follow the road and the balises (on trees, rocks, pylons, fences, buildings etc.) as it winds (mostly) up and (sometimes) down, past small roadside farms. At fork bear L. KSO following road all the time *(but keep turning round from time to time to admire the view - there is nothing as long or as steep until you climb up to El Cebreiro in the Montes de León, by which time you will be fit and ready for it, if you aren't already). At this level there are still trees to provide some shade.* Pass a T-junction *(Maison Etchébestia, 302m)*, and KSO. Watch out for occasional vehicles. 100m further on, road forks at massive tree *(good place for a rest)* - keep R *(fork to L goes down to village of Saint Michel)*.

By now you will also see the occasional yellow flashes or "flechas" - the waymarking system used on the camino in Spain.

50m after passing the hamlet of *Honto* (540m) the road veers R but the GR65 bears L up a grassy track (the old road), leaving the modern road for a while (to rejoin it later) making a short cut via the old, steep route that zigzags between walls/banks at first and then on open ground. The "balises" are mainly painted on rocks on the ground in this section but if you have difficulty in seeing them (eg. in snow) you can spot the place where you will meet the road again a) by a tap on the RH side of the road and b) by two small houses L and R of the road - the one on your R is called *Arbol Azopian*. The path joins the road again (at 710m) after eight to nine hairpins.

[NB: if you are walking <u>to</u> Saint Jean Pied-de-Port, ie. going back, leave the road to your <u>R</u> after the tap on your <u>L</u>, dropping down by a drystone wall and walking alongside it. This turn is well marked on a large rock at RH side of the road before you leave it.]

From here you can see over the mountains to the east towards the Col de Somport, Mont d'Aspe etc., snow-covered (peaks) for much of the year. KSO on road, ignoring tracks to either L or R. When you see a farm building off to the L where a stream crosses under the road, the road veers round to the R and shortly afterwards, after three to four more hairpins, the road flattens out and you reach the

12km Vierge d'Orisson 1,095m

A small statue of the Virgin Mary in a prominent position at the side of a road junction and in a level area. Panoramic views and a good place for a

rest (not too long). At the Vierge d'Orisson you are halfway in time (but not in distance) between Saint Jean Pied-de-Port and Roncesvalles. It is still 6km to the border and the route still climbs, though less steeply now, up to the Col de Bentarte, after which it is nearly all downhill. The temperature may be cooler as you climb higher but the sun, if it is out, will still be as hot.

Take the R fork here and continue on road (having taken R fork) and KSO at road junction (with the D128 (R) to Arnéguy). At 1177m pass the "remains" of Château Pignon (L). Ignore a turn to L after 300m and also a fork to R after 300m (to a farm 100m off road).

Continue on road until it begins to veer round to L, at which point the camino leaves the road (at 1240m) up a well waymarked grassy track (balises, flechas and three scallop shells on a signpost to the R), towards a pass above you on the rocky summit of *Leizar-Atheka* (1,300m). Since the road veers L you are in effect continuing more or less in a straight line, although you actually walk off the road to the R. *(The road itself continues for another 3km to the Col d'Arnostéguy, more or less on the level, before it comes to a dead end.)*

Climb up between the two very large rocks, after which the path begins to descend. Pass border marker stone number 198 (1,290m) and then follow the border fence (above the forest below you to the R) to marker no. 199 (1,344m). 20m after this you cross a cattle grid through the fence into

4km Spain
You may find remains of snow here, even in early June.

The grassy track veers round to the R, past a tumbledown house (L) at the *Col de Bentarte* (1330m). Continue along path through beechwoods, for 3-4km. Pass sheep pen and hut on R̲. Do not take R fork here but KSO back into the woods again (well waymarked).

When you come out of the woods again the track falls away to the R *(good views)* but KSO (ie. don't fork R here). 10m further on track forks left but KSO (ie. take R fork). *(Over to your L you will now be able to see the TV mast on Monte Orzanzurieta, 1,570m.)* From here the path winds (mostly) up for 1-2km to meet the road at the

4km Col Lepoeder 1430m
From here you have the first, plunging, view of the rooftops of the abbey at

Roncesvalles down in the valley below, the village of Burguete and, on a clear day, right across into the province of Navarra.

There are in fact two routes down to Roncesvalles but the first is very steep.

The **Calzada Romana** (old Roman road) is very steep and drops down to the monastery directly, straight ahead, avoiding the Puerta d'Ibañeta or the Col de Roncesvaux (1057m). This is reportedly well-waymarked, if you are able to find them, and passes to the L of the hill known as Don Simon.

The alternative is to follow the road, which you join by taking a short path R off the road you are on after the Col and follow it down (there are a few short cuts through its hairpins) to the

4km Puerto d'Ibañeta

This is where Charlemagne had got to when he heard Roland blow his horn, too late to go back to help him. A bell used to toll at the original chapel to guide pilgrims in bad weather. A modern ermita (chapel) was built in 1965 to replace the earlier ruined chapel of Charlemagne, with a sign in French, Spanish, Basque and Latin inviting pilgrims to pray to N-D de Roncevaux. There is also a modern monument to Roland (Roldán in Spanish) of Chanson de Roland fame.

From here you walk through the woods for the last 2km to **Roncesvalles**, gently downhill. The track is waymarked (yellow arrow on side of building to L of road just before you reach the chapel). Shortly before you get to the abbey you are joined by a track coming from the L, after which you enter the rear of the monastery (*fountain*). Cross diagonally through a courtyard and pass in front of the church.

The Route Napoléon is also practicable on a mountain bike if you are prepared to dismount occasionally, eg. after Honto on the short-cut section and near the border but there should be no problem with a sturdy machine. Touring bikes could also manage it if they did not take the short cut at Honto but remained on the road and if their riders were prepared to push along all the non-tarred sections - some 7-8km. On a clear day it would definitely be worth the effort.

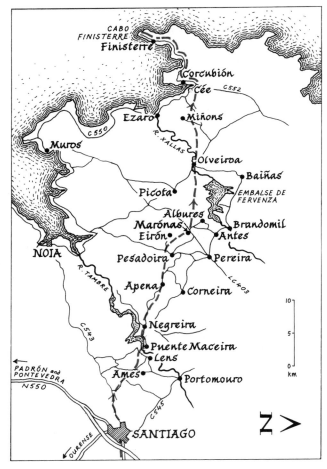

MAP 10

APPENDIX B - SANTIAGO TO FINISTERRE

Finisterre ("Fisterra" in Gallego) was the end of the known world until Columbus altered things, and was the final destination of many of the pilgrims who made the journey to Santiago in centuries gone by. It is still possible to walk there avoiding main roads though not many people do at present, perhaps because of lack of information and route-finding difficulties.

The route described here leads 85km due west from Santiago, in roughly a straight line, along footpaths, quiet roads and country lanes and is waymarked for the most part. However, as there is no single definitive route and as there are frequently (waymarked) variants to choose from, which meet up again later on, what follows is not a description of all the many possibilities but a guide to one route which should be easy to follow and pleasant to walk. Allow three days to walk to Finisterre, with possible overnight stops in Negreira and Cée, though this will mean a <u>very</u> long second day. The actual walking isn't hard but there are a lot of climbs and descents.

The route to Finisterre differs from the main camino in a number of ways, one of which is the *waymarking*. This is done with the familiar yellow arrows but here they point in both directions, not only <u>towards</u> Santiago but back again as well. From time to time you will also find that while turnings are waymarked ahead of time they are not indicated at the turn itself. Likewise, when you turn left, for example, you may be confronted with a choice of two (or more) further options, the correct one not waymarked until a certain distance along it.

Some *maps* are available in Santiago bookshops, such as the 1:250.000 map of Galicia (published by the Xunta de Galicia) and the relevant sheets of the 1:25.000 series of the Mapa Topográfico Nacional de España ("hojas" 93-1, 93-2 and 92-2). The latter cover the most difficult parts of the route but are by no means infallible when searching for minor roads and tracks as they do not indicate even all the tarred roads or give the names of the villages on them. The spellings of *place names* may vary, too, On signposts they will be in Gallego (Galician), on some maps in Castilian, but as definitive spellings for the latter have not yet been settled these too may appear in more than one version.

Very many villages are also so small that they are not marked with their names at either entrance or exit so unless you ask (and meet someone you can ask) you may not always know exactly where you are. If, on occasion, you do think you are lost, retrace your steps to the previous waymark as once you have picked up the first one in Puente Maceira, they do, in fact, lead you all the way to the town of Finisterre itself, apart from a few places (indicated in the text).

If/when you do need to ask the way you will need to know in advance the name of the <u>next</u> village you want to pass through, asking your way from one to another as the medieval pilgrims did. However, as many people may assume you want to get to Finisterre as quickly as possible they may direct you to the main road. You will then have to explain that you want to go along the old tracks and assess the reliability of the information given you, according to whether the person has actually been that way himself or just heard about it. It will be obvious from this that your Spanish needs to be reasonably good, all the more so since although you ask your question in Castilian the answer may well be given in Gallego...

Accommodation is readily available in Negreira, Cée, Corcubión and Finisterre itself but in between there is a long gap (some 50km) between Negreira and Cée. Elsewhere there is nothing at all, at present anyway.

Food: you will pass some shops and bars along the way but it is better to take at least some reserve supplies with you.

From the above it might seem that the prospect is somewhat daunting but it is definitely worth it. Finisterre is the real end of the journey, both in the physical sense and in the religious and historical one. The scenery is beautiful, it is very peaceful and there are, at present, very few walkers so the route is very different from the main camino before Santiago. It is often wet in this part of Spain but you will have the opportunity to see something of the real Galicia, away from the big towns. You can return to Santiago by bus, either direct or with a change in Vimianze, every day except Sunday.

The Route

To leave Santiago you initially make for the church of *San Lorenzo (San Lourenzo de Trasouto)* on the western outskirts of the town. A pleasant way to get there is to cross the big Santa Susanna park *(Carballeira de Santa Susanna)*, heading for the university buildings. Veer R after passing the older buildings, on to the *Avenida de Burgos*, which joins up with the *Calle San Lourenzo*. Pass the church of *San Lorenzo* and KSO until you reach the junction with the main road in

2km Vidan

Turn R and continue along main road to

4km Roxos

Go through village and turn R at bridge *(café)* up a hill signposted to "Portomouro 12". KSO to village of

2km Aquapesada

Turn L at junction at bottom of hill in village and pass bar after 150m. Turn R 50m after *bar* onto road signposted "Trasmonte 3, 5 P. Maceira". KSO, uphill all the time, through eucalyptus woods *(fountain on R 100m before top)* to

3km Trasmonte

Bar/shop. Continue on road to

2km Puente Maceira

Picturesque village with stone bridge over the River Tambre, with small but wide waterfall. Cross bridge (*Capilla San Blas* at end) and then turn L at end of village *(fountain on R but may not be drinkable)*. The yellow arrows start here. Go L at fork and L again onto a minor road which becomes a track and continues through fields and woods, returning to the river bank. Go under the road bridge over the river and KSO along the bank. Continue on track joining from R (road) and KSO again through fields.

Rejoin the road again after 1km but turn L off it after 500m at signpost to "Logrosa 3" (river to your L). KSO. *Eucalyptus and other woods.* At top of hill enter village of

5km Chancela
KSO(L) at junction and then KSO(R) at the next one. Turn L at the bottom of the hill and enter

2km Negreira
All facilities.

Go uphill, veering R, into town and then turn L (Hostal Mezquito on corner) down main street. Continue along it to the bottom, passing under arches (fountain in public garden to R) and KSO on road, crossing the bridge at the end of the town. At a junction turn R, signposted to "Outes 15. Marco del Cornado 14.5" and continue uphill to the village of

2km Zas (Xas)
Turn R here at junction off the main road and follow a more minor road round until it veers sharp L. Do not fork R down a lane but KSO ahead along another lane which almost immediately forks into two. Take the L of these, although it is not waymarked straight away, and KSO for 1km or so through the woods, along a fairly clear track with (old) waymarks on trees etc. from time to time. Turn L when you reach a T junction with a walled field ahead of you along a lane past a school until you reach the road.

Turn R along it into an unmarked hamlet. KSO and pass another unmarked one after 1km and then turn R off the road down a grassy track through fields. Cross a minor road after 15m and KSO through the village of **Rabote**. Turn L at end down a green lane (field to your R) and follow it for 500m to the valley bottom. Turn R at the T junction at the bottom and then continue uphill up a walled lane (overgrown) through an old oak forest. After approx. 1km you will emerge, after a two or three zigzags, onto the road above the village of

5km A Pena (Peña)
Bar. KSO along road through the hamlet of **Porto Camino**, ignoring yellow arrows to L and R. Continue until you reach the beginning of the village of

4km Vilaserio

Immediately before the first house at the approach to the village turn L off the road down a walled lane and then L again at the end after 50m onto the road into the village. Fork R and then turn R again onto a minor road parallel to the one you have turned off, which is now over to your R. KSO down to a T junction and turn L here (not waymarked) uphill again to **Quintela** (200m), continuing uphill again for 300m further to **Pedrouzo** and then, after 500m, enter village of

4km Pesadoira

2 bars. Cross road and KSO down minor road for 4km in a dead straight line (it eventually becomes a track), ignoring any turnings to R or L until you reach the main road. (This part is not waymarked.) Turn L along the road (a lot of traffic) and enter village of

2km Maroñas

A very long, straggling village. Bar, shop (ask for it) and bar/restaurant.

KSO through village, ignoring any waymarks you may see to the L (apparently there are several sets, not all of which are correct) past the bar/restaurant Casa Victoriana. Turn R up a minor road 300m further on, signposted "Buenjesus. Guiema. Vilar de Castro". Follow this road round to the L, uphill to the village of

2km Gueima

Turn R down a minor road which leads downhill. At the bottom turn L uphill again by a lavadero (outdoor washplace). At the top of the hill, at the 2nd R turn, you will see two sets of waymarks. (The turn to the R down a lane is a variant route and apparently meets up again with the main one at Cée.) KSO on road (also waymarked) downhill.

2km Lago

At the bottom take the 2nd R downhill and then KSO (L) at next fork in small village of **Abeleiroas** (1km). KSO on road (very little traffic) at next fork *(bar?)*. Halfway up the hill turn R by a bus shelter and KSO down a minor road, ignoring turns to L and R for 3kms to

4km San Cristóbal de Corzen
Pass church and cemetery and turn L at junction. KSO to next village and turn R at junction onto larger road (café). Cross the bridge over the River *Xallas* and enter

1km Puente Olveiroa (Olveira)
KSO on main road (which veers L for 2km and then, after passing a turning to R to "Santiago Olveiros" turn L off main road onto a minor and go through the village of

3km Olveiroa (Olveira)
Here there are a lot of "horreos". Church over to L, bar 50m uphill to R.
Turn L at end of village onto main road again. After 100m there is a waymarked turning to the L, which leads along the side of a lake (up to Logos) but is so overgrown at present as to be impossible to use. Instead, continue uphill (very steep) on the road.

At the top (3km) there is a wayside crucifix on the RH side and you will see two large, ugly factories ahead of you on the skyline: this is the village of Hospital. Below you, to the L, is Logos, which is less easy to enter than it might seem initially because the turning L down a minor road is just a section of the old road (before it was straightened out) and merely leads you back again to the main road. Turn L down it but then, after 20m, turn L again off it at what looks like the entrance to an old lane. Cross two fields, go L round the edge of the second one and then down a lane through woods in the direction of Logos. When you reach a junction fork R down another lane, cross bridge over a river and enter village of

5km Logos
Here you will pick up the waymarks again. Follow them through village and then out of it, leaving it behind you to your R. (Waymarks stop again here.) Turn R at first fork and R again, 400m later, uphill, at second fork. Continue uphill all the time, aiming for an enormous T-shaped dolmen-like group of stones about 15 feet high. Waymarks begin again. *(When the track levels out you will have the factories ahead of you again.)* Continue along the track (nearly all the way to Hospital) until you reach a T junction. Turn L and KSO down to the road, turning hard R up it to village of

Stone formations near Logos

View towards Finisterre

4km Anséan

Here the waymarks point you to the L but they fizzle out 1km further on in Xestosa. Instead, turn R along minor road for 2km to a junction with the main road to Finisterre (*bar*). Turn L along it and follow it as it winds it way downhill all the time to

10km Cée

Coastal town with all facilities.

Just before you enter the town (at its name board) a yellow arrow leads you through a small complex of flats towards the sea and then alongside the beach. Rejoin the road again and enter

1km Corcubión

All facilities.

Follow the main road (signposted "Fisterra") uphill out of town for 3km (it zigzags a lot but there appear to be no short cuts) until you reach a large play/picnic area and tennis court at the top, where the road turns sharp R. KSO straight ahead here, down a minor road (waymarked) and then turn R immediately down a green lane (not waymarked straight away). Veer L along wall and past fuente. This cuts out quite a long section of road before you return to it again at a red bus shelter.

Fork L 200m further on (on road) down a FP into the woods (watch out for waymarks on trees), pine at first and then eucalyptus.

When you reach a junction at the bottom (field and stone wall to L, sea ahead of you) turn R (the path you were on turns sharp L here). This too is not waymarked immediately but there are yellow flashes on the ground later on. Follow this path slightly uphill until you rejoin the road. Continue along it to

7km Sardiñeiro
Shops, bars, campsite.

Here yellow arrows lead you off the main road onto quieter streets near the sea: turn L alongside football pitch *(Rua de Playa)* and continue along *Rua de Marina* between main road and sea. Turn L onto main road at end of village and KSO along it, entering woods again, until you reach the hamlet of

5km Anchoa
Turn L down minor road opposite "autoservicio" (shop) and café and then turn R. When you reach a small "roundabout" head for the beach and continue along it to the buildings at the end. *Bar/ restaurant in the somewhat grandly named "Calle San Roque": presumably this was once a much bigger place, referring, as it does, to the saint associated with pilgrims. The beach here is strewn with literally thousands of shells, scallop and others, recalling the legend of the equestrian bridegroom.*

Go up track to L of bar (waymarked) and KSO(L) along road at top by tall wayside crucifix into

2km Finisterre
Small fishing port with all facilities.

From here it is a further 2km along the road to the lighthouse (el faro), uphill past the church of *Santa María (Romanesque in part with a statue of Saint James).* This is the real "land's end" and is clearly signposted. *(Fountain on RH side of road at sharp LH bend.) As the weather is often misty until about midday in this part of Spain you may have better views from here in the late afternoon and evening.*

APPENDIX C - OUTLINE GUIDE TO THE "CAMINO MOZARABE" OR "VÍA DE LA PLATA"

As explained in the introduction, there was not just one "Camino de Santiago" but several, one of which was the "Camino mozárabe" or "Vía de la Plata," so-named, according to one theory at least, because it followed the old Roman silver road from Huelva in the south to Astorga. This was the route taken by pilgrims from southern Spain, once the reconquest of Seville had taken place and led north, in more or less a straight line, via Seville, Zafra, Mérida, Cáceres, Salamanca and Zamora until it joined the "Camino francés" in Astorga. It has recently been waymarked with yellow arrows and is easy to follow but as yet not many people take it, presumably because, as a walk, it is still not very well known. There is no guide to it either, apart from (in Spanish) four very practical articles, with sketch plans, by the late Andrés Muñoz Garde in issues 15-16, 17, 23 and 24-25 of the magazine Peregrino (Nov. 1990, Dec. 1990, Dec. 1991 and April 1992).

However, since the the Vía de la Plata is easy to follow (it is not a "map-and-compass" walk) and until a full-scale walkers' guide is published a skeleton outline is given here to enable (and encourage) interested people to undertake it. This contains a list of the places, large and small, through which this camino passes, and should be used in conjunction with Michelin maps 446 (Southern Spain), 444 (Central Spain) and 441 (Galicia/Asturias-León).

The route is very varied, both in climate, scenery, history and architecture (you are very much aware of being in Roman Spain) and differs from the northern road in a number of practical ways. It is much warmer (July and August are definitely not recommended) and the best time is either April-May or in the autumn. In the south there is very little water (and very few fountains, though fortunately these increase in number and reliability the farther north you go) so you will usually have to carry everything you need for the entire day. In Andalucía and some parts of Extremadura there are a lot of very large properties (farms known as "cortijos") and very few tracks or roads other than the main road so that in some places this unavoidably coincides with the camino. Later, though, you may spend complete days in the countryside on old tracks, never meeting a single person or passing a single village from morning to evening.

You are also unlikely to meet many, if any, other walkers and for this reason some people may prefer to go with a companion.

Not only is the route well waymarked from the outskirts of Seville but the tracks/lanes themselves are very clear and obvious, with none of the "sendas" or very small footpaths sometimes encountered on the "Camino francés". However, unlike the northern route, the existence of the Vía de la Plata as a walk is almost unknown amongst the people who live along its path, including priests, policemen and people who have yellow arrows a few yards from their front doors, so that if you have trouble, for example, finding your way <u>out</u> of a place you will need (as well as good Spanish) to know the name of some prominent building/street/ other feature near its exit so that you can ask for that instead. It is therefore a good idea to go for a "paseo" in the evening to check where you will leave from the following morning; in small places this is not usually too difficult, since the Vía de la Plata heads north all the time, but in bigger towns it can be more complicated, especially if there have been roadworks.

How long does it take? The distance between Seville and Astorga is approximately 690km so the amount of time you need will depend on your pace, stamina and the number of rest days you want to take. A month is probably a minimum, plus another nine or ten days if you want to continue on from Astorga to Santiago.

Language. A working (or better) knowledge of Spanish is even more essential on the Vía de la Plata than on the Camino francés and regional accents may be particularly difficult to follow. In Andalucía, for instance, and in parts of Extremadura, all the intervocalic and terminal "s's" disappear from words so that, as an example, "dos meses" ("two months") will sound like "doh may".

Accommodation. There are no refuges along the Vía de la Plata and in some places (eg. between Cáceres and Salamanca) there are very long stretches without any accommodation within even unreasonable walking distance. However, places of any size, particularly if they are on a main road, usually have some kind of facilities, if only "camas" in bars for "camioneros" (lorry drivers) and which are often surprisingly good value.

Getting there. a) By air direct to Seville from London (Iberia has scheduled flights). b) By train. There is now a high-speed train (the TAV or AVE) from Madrid to Seville via Córdoba. c) By coach, either direct to Seville from London or via Madrid, from where long-distance buses are also available to Mérida, Cáceres, Salamanca and Zamora.

The Route

Figures after place names refer, respectively, to the distance from Seville and the number of kilometres remaining to Astorga, and, where known, a place's height (in metres) and its population. Thus, for example, Camas 5/685 is 5km from Seville and 685 from Astorga.

	Seville	0/690	(12m, 650,000)
5km	Camas	5/685	(13m)
4km	Santiponce	9/681	(16m)
15km	Gerena	24/663	(99m, 4000)
12km	El Garrobo	36/654	(267m)
3.5km	Venta del Alto	39.5/650.5	(350m)
16.5km	El Ronquillo	56/634	(334m)
23km	Santa Olalla del Cala	79/611	(539m)
11km	Casilla de los Conejos	90/600	
4km	Venta del Culebrin	94/596	
3km	La Nava	97/593	
6km	Monasterio	103/587	(760m)
19km	Fuente de Cantos	122/568	(586m)
6km	Calzadilla de los Barrios	128/562	(556m)
14km	La Puebla de Sancho Pérez	142/548	(530m)
3.5km	Zafra	145.5/544.5	(510m, 12,900)
4.5km	Los Santos de Maimona	150/540	(8100)
18km	Villafranca de los Barrios	168/522	(425m)
13km	Almendralejo (off route)		(340m, 23,600)
13km	Torremegía	189/501	(302m)

15km	Mérida	204/486	(218m, 51,000)
15km	El Carrascalejo	219/471	(303m)
2.5km	Aljucén	221.5/468.5	(230m)
14.5km	Cruz del Niño Muerto	236/454	
5km	Alcuéscar	241/449	(489m)
8km	Casa de Don Antonio	249/441	(413m)
7km	Aldea del Cano	256/434	(396m)
12km	Valdesalor	268/422	(380m)
12km	Cáceres	280/410	(464m 69,193)
12km	Casar de Cáceres	292/398	(369m)
19km	Apeadero del Río Tajo	311/379	
15km	Cañaveral	326/364	(360m, 2100)
7km	Grimaldo	333/357	(480m)
19km	San Gil	352/338	(271m)
20km	Venta Quemada	372/318	
6km	Cáparra	378/312	
19km	Aldeanueva del Camino	397/293	(530m)
11km	Baños de Montemayor	408/282	(710m)
12km	Calzada de Béjar	420/270	(796m)
9km	Valdelacasa	429/261	(964m)
8km	Fuenterroble de Salvatierra	437/253	(982m)
10km	Navarredonda de la Sierra	447/243	(982m)
5km	Pico de la Dueña	452/238	(1,170m)
8km	Calzadilla de Mendigos	460/230	(950m)
7km	San Pedro de Rozados	467/223	(980m)
22km	Salamanca	489/201	(800m, 167,000)
6km	Aldeaseca	495/195	(820m)
5km	Castellanos de Villiquiera	500/190	(830m)
4km	Calzada de Valdunciel	504/186	(807m)
5km	Apeadero de Huelmos	509/181	
14km	El Cubo de Tierra del Vino	523/167	(846m)

13km	Villanueva de Campeán	536/154	(765m)
6km	San Marcial	542/148	(740m)
14km	Zamora	556/134	(655m, 57,734)
6km	Roales de Pan	562/128	(700m)
12km	Montamarta	574/116	(690m)
10km	Fontanilles de Castro	584/106	(725m)
4km	Riego del Camino	588/102	(705m)
6km	Granja de Moruela	594/96	(708m)
9km	Santovenia	603/87	(715m)
5km	Villaveza del Agua	608/82	(700m)
2km	Barcial del Barco	610/80	(717m)
5km	Castropepe	615/75	(720m)
8km	Benavente	623/67	(745m, 12,500)
8km	Villabrázaro	631/59	(710m)
9km	Maire de Castroponce	640/50	(748m)
5km	Alija del Infantado	645/45	(740m)
4km	La Nora del Río	649/41	(730m)
2km	Navianos	651/39	(732m)
7km	San Juan de Torres	658/32	(730m)
8km	La Bañeza	666/24	(777m, 8501)
2km	Santiago de la Valduerna	668/22	(775m)
3km	Palacios de la Valduerna	671/19	
14km	Cuevas	685/05	(840m)
5km	Astorga	690/00	(869m, 14,000)

APPENDIX D - GLOSSARY

alcázar	fortress, castle
aldea	hamlet
alto	hill, height
arroyo	stream, small river
ayuntamiento	town hall
barrio	suburb
bascula	weighbridge
bodega	wine cellar; also used to describe a store place for wine located in hillsides and other places in the open countryside.
cafetería	a café that also serves snacks (not a self-service restaurant for hot meals)
calzada	(paved) road, causeway
camino	track, path
capilla	chapel
carretera	(main) road, highway
casa consistorial	town hall in small places
cigüeña	stork
clédo	gate made of paling fence
desvía	detour, diversion (eg. on roads)
embalse	dam, reservoir
ermita	hermitage, small chapel
finca	smallholding
fonda	guest house, inn
frontón	pelota court
fuente	fountain, spring
gallego	Galician
horreo	(raised) granary
hospedaje	a fonda (in Galicia)
hospedería	inn, hostelry

hostal	hotel (less expensive than a hotel)
igrexia	church (Galician)
jacobeo	(adj.) of Saint James
meseta	plateau, tableland
mesón	restaurant (often simple, with period decor)
palloza	round thatched dwelling of Celtic origin
palmero	pilgrim who has been to Jerusalem
panadería	bakery
pantano	marsh, swamp (natural); reservoir, dam (artificial)
páramo	plain, bleak plateau (often used in place names)
paseo	stroll, walk; avenue
peregrino	pilgrim
posada	inn (simpler than a fonda)
pueblo	village, small town
puente	bridge
puerta	door, gateway (esp. fig., often found in place names)
puerto	mountain pass; port
rollo	stone wayside cross, often at junctions; raised up and may be highly decorated
rodeo	roundabout or indirect route
romería	pilgrimage to a local shrine
romero	pilgrim (originally one who had been to Rome)
rúa	street (Galician)
sellar	to (rubber) stamp
sello	stamp, seal
senda	(small) path, track
señal	waymark, signal
sirga	camino

| tapas | light snack taken with drinks in a bar |
| vega | fertile plain, lowland area, valley (often found in place names) |

BIBLIOGRAPHY

Pierre Barret & Jean-Noël Gurgand, *Priez pour nous à Compostelle*,
  Paris: Hachette, 1978.
  An account of the authors' journey from Vézelay to Santiago
  on foot, interspersed with parallel accounts of pilgrims from
  previous centuries. Contains a very extensive bibliography.

Laurie Dennett, *A hug for the apostle. On foot from Chartres to
  Santiago de Compostela*, Toronto: Macmillan of Canada, 1987.
  An account of the author's walk, undertaken to raise money
  for the Multiple Sclerosis Society. Although some of the book
  covers the pilgrimage in France much of it is devoted to the
  route in Spain, including much interesting historical material.

Michael Jacobs, *The Road to Santiago de Compostela* (Architectural
  Guides for Travellers series), London: Viking 1990.
  A guide to the churches, monasteries, hostels and hospitals
  along the pilgrim route, analysing their architectural styles.
  Contains photos, maps and detailed plans.

Edward Mullins, *The Pilgrimage to Santiago*, London: Secker &
  Warburg, 1974.
  An account of the art, architecture, history and geography of
  the pilgrim route from Paris to Santiago.

Rob Neillands, *The Road to Compostela*, Ashbourne: Moorland
  Publishing Co., 1985.
  An account of the author's journey from Le Puy to Santiago
  by bicycle.

Walter Starkie, *The Road to Santiago. Pilgrim of St. James*, London:
  John Murray, 1957.
  An account of a pilgrimage to Santiago, part travel, part
  history, part autobiography.

Brian and Marcus Tate, *The Pilgrim Route to Santiago*, Oxford:
  Phaidon, 1987.

Explains the pilgrim phenomenon and the history of the shrine as well as discussing the different routes. Contains 137 photographic illustrations by Pablo Keller, 50 of them in colour.

Jeanne Viellard, *Guide du Pèlerin de Saint Jacques de Compostelle*, Paris: Klincksieck, 4th edn 1989.
A French translation, on facing pages, of what is probably the first known guidebook: Aymery Picaud's twelfth-century description of the pilgrim routes to Santiago.

Peregrino magazine, 6 issues a year, articles (general, historical, practical accounts of journeys) on the pilgrimage.

The Pilgrim's Guide: a 12th century Guide for the Pilgrim to St. James of Compostela, translated from the Latin by James Hogarth, Confraternity of Saint James, 1992.

Song of Roland, translated by G.Burgess, Penguin Classics, 1990.

Useful Addresses

Confraternity of St. James,
45 Dolben Street,
London SE1 0UQ.

Los Amigos del Camino de Santiago,
Apartado de Correos 20,
Estella,
Navarra, Spain.

Peregrino, Boletin del Camino de Santiago,
Apartado 60,
26250 Santo Domingo de la Calzada,
La Rioja, Spain.

NOTES

CICERONE GUIDES

Cicerone publish a wide range of reliable guides to walking and climbing in Britain, and other general interest books.

LAKE DISTRICT - General Books
A DREAM OF EDEN
LAKELAND VILLAGES
LAKELAND TOWNS
REFLECTIONS ON THE LAKES
OUR CUMBRIA
THE HIGH FELLS OF LAKELAND
CONISTON COPPER A History
LAKELAND - A taste to remember (Recipes)
THE LOST RESORT? (Morecambe)
CHRONICLES OF MILNTHORPE
LOST LANCASHIRE (Furness area)
THE PRIORY OF CARTMEL

LAKE DISTRICT - Guide Books
CASTLES IN CUMBRIA
THE CUMBRIA CYCLE WAY
WESTMORLAND HERITAGE WALK
IN SEARCH OF WESTMORLAND
CONISTON COPPER MINES Field Guide
SCRAMBLES IN THE LAKE DISTRICT
MORE SCRAMBLES IN THE LAKE DISTRICT
SHORT WALKS - SOUTH LAKELAND
WINTER CLIMBS IN THE LAKE DISTRICT
WALKS IN SILVERDALE/ARNSIDE
BIRDS OF MORECAMBE BAY
THE EDEN WAY
WALKING ROUND THE LAKES

NORTHERN ENGLAND (outside the Lakes
BIRDWATCHING ON MERSEYSIDE
CANAL WALKS Vol 1 North
CANOEISTS GUIDE TO THE NORTH EAST
THE CLEVELAND WAY & MISSING LINK
THE DALES WAY
DOUGLAS VALLEY WAY
HADRIANS WALL Vol 1 The Wall Walk
HERITAGE TRAILS IN NW ENGLAND
THE ISLE OF MAN COASTAL PATH
IVORY TOWERS & DRESSED STONES (Follies)
THE LANCASTER CANAL
LANCASTER CANAL WALKS
LAUGHS ALONG THE PENNINE WAY
A NORTHERN COAST-TO-COAST
NORTH YORK MOORS Walks
THE REIVERS WAY (Northumberland)
THE RIBBLE WAY
ROCK CLIMBS LANCASHIRE & NW
THE YORKSHIRE DALES A walker's guide
WALKING IN THE SOUTH PENNINES
WALKING IN THE NORTH PENNINES
WALKS IN THE YORKSHIRE DALES (3 VOL)
WALKS IN LANCASHIRE WITCH COUNTRY
WALKS IN THE NORTH YORK MOORS
WALKS TO YORKSHIRE WATERFALLS (2 vol)
WALKS ON THE WEST PENNINE MOORS
WALKING NORTHERN RAILWAYS (2 vol)
WALKING IN THE WOLDS

DERBYSHIRE & EAST MIDLANDS
WHITE PEAK WALKS - 2 Vols
HIGH PEAK WALKS
WHITE PEAK WAY
KINDER LOG
THE VIKING WAY
THE DEVIL'S MILL / WHISTLING CLOUGH (Novels)

WALES & WEST MIDLANDS
THE RIDGES OF SNOWDONIA
HILLWALKING IN SNOWDONIA
HILL WALKING IN WALES (2 Vols)
ASCENT OF SNOWDON
WELSH WINTER CLIMBS
SNOWDONIA WHITE WATER SEA & SURF
SCRAMBLES IN SNOWDONIA
SARN HELEN Walking Roman Road
ROCK CLIMBS IN WEST MIDLANDS
THE SHROPSHIRE HILLS A Walker's Guide
HEREFORD & THE WYE VALLEY A Walker's Guide
THE WYE VALLEY WALK

SOUTH & SOUTH WEST ENGLAND
COTSWOLD WAY
EXMOOR & THE QUANTOCKS
THE KENNET & AVON WALK
THE SOUTHERN-COAST-TO-COAST
SOUTH DOWNS WAY & DOWNS LINK
SOUTH WEST WAY - 2 Vol
WALKING IN THE CHILTERNS
WALKING ON DARTMOOR
WALKERS GUIDE TO DARTMOOR PUBS
WALKS IN KENT
THE WEALDWAY & VANGUARD WAY

SCOTLAND
THE BORDER COUNTRY - WALKERS GUIDE
SCRAMBLES IN LOCHABER
SCRAMBLES IN SKYE
THE ISLAND OF RHUM
CAIRNGORMS WINTER CLIMBS
THE CAIRNGORM GLENS (Mountainbike Guide)
THE ATHOLL GLENS (Mountainbike Guide)
WINTER CLIMBS BEN NEVIS & GLENCOE
SCOTTISH RAILWAY WALKS
TORRIDON A Walker's Guide
SKI TOURING IN SCOTLAND

REGIONAL BOOKS UK & IRELAND
THE MOUNTAINS OF ENGLAND & WALES
    VOL 1 WALES VOL 2 ENGLAND
THE MOUNTAINS OF IRELAND
THE ALTERNATIVE PENNINE WAY
THE PACKHORSE BRIDGES OF ENGLAND
THE RELATIVE HILLS OF BRITAIN
LIMESTONE - 100 BEST CLIMBS

Also a full range of EUROPEAN and OVERSEAS guidebooks - walking, long distance trails, scrambling, ice-climbing, rock climbing.

Other guides are constantly being added to the Cicerone List.
Available from bookshops, outdoor equipment shops or direct (send s.a.e. for price list) from
CICERONE, 2 POLICE SQUARE, MILNTHORPE, CUMBRIA, LA7 7PY

CICERONE GUIDES

Cicerone publish a wide range of reliable guides to walking and climbing abroad

FRANCE
TOUR OF MONT BLANC
CHAMONIX MONT BLANC - A Walking Guide
TOUR OF THE OISANS: GR54
WALKING THE FRENCH ALPS: GR5
THE CORSICAN HIGH LEVEL ROUTE: GR20
THE WAY OF ST JAMES: GR65
THE PYRENEAN TRAIL: GR10
THE RLS (Stevenson) TRAIL
TOUR OF THE QUEYRAS
ROCK CLIMBS IN THE VERDON
WALKS IN VOLCANO COUNTRY (Auvergne)
WALKING THE FRENCH GORGES (Provence)
FRENCH ROCK

FRANCE / SPAIN
WALKS AND CLIMBS IN THE PYRENEES
ROCK CLIMBS IN THE PYRENEES

SPAIN
WALKS & CLIMBS IN THE PICOS DE EUROPA
WALKING IN MALLORCA
BIRDWATCHING IN MALLORCA
COSTA BLANCA CLIMBS
ANDALUSIAN ROCK CLIMBS
THE WAY OF ST JAMES

FRANCE / SWITZERLAND
THE JURA - Walking the High Route and
   Winter Ski Traverses
CHAMONIX TO ZERMATT The Walker's
   Haute Route

SWITZERLAND
WALKING IN THE BERNESE ALPS
CENTRAL SWITZERLAND
WALKS IN THE ENGADINE
WALKING IN TICINO
THE VALAIS - A Walking Guide
THE ALPINE PASS ROUTE

GERMANY / AUSTRIA / EASTERN EUROPE
THE KALKALPEN TRAVERSE
KLETTERSTEIG - Scrambles
WALKING IN THE BLACK FOREST
MOUNTAIN WALKING IN AUSTRIA
WALKING IN THE HARZ MOUNTAINS
WALKING IN THE SALZKAMMERGUT
KING LUDWIG WAY
HUT-TO-HUT IN THE STUBAI ALPS
THE HIGH TATRAS

ITALY & SLOVENIA
ALTA VIA - High Level Walkis in the Dolomites
VIA FERRATA - Scrambles in the Dolomites
ITALIAN ROCK - Rock Climbs in Northern Italy
CLASSIC CLIMBS IN THE DOLOMITES
WALKING IN THE DOLOMITES
THE JULIAN ALPS

MEDITERRANEAN COUNTRIES
THE MOUNTAINS OF GREECE
CRETE: Off the beaten track
TREKS & CLIMBS IN WADI RUM, JORDAN
THE ATLAS MOUNTAINS
WALKS & CLIMBS IN THE ALA DAG (Turkey)

OTHER COUNTRIES
ADVENTURE TREKS - W. N. AMERICA
ADVENTURE TREKS - NEPAL
ANNAPURNA TREKKERS GUIDE
CLASSIC TRAMPS IN NEW ZEALAND
TREKKING IN THE CAUCASUS

GENERAL OUTDOOR BOOKS
THE HILL WALKERS MANUAL
FIRST AID FOR HILLWALKERS
MOUNTAIN WEATHER
MOUNTAINEERING LITERATURE
THE ADVENTURE ALTERNATIVE
MODERN ALPINE CLIMBING
ROPE TECHNIQUES IN MOUNTAINEERING
MODERN SNOW & ICE TECHNIQUES
LIMESTONE -100 BEST CLIMBS IN BRITAIN

CANOEING
SNOWDONIA WILD WATER, SEA & SURF
WILDWATER CANOEING
CANOEIST'S GUIDE TO THE NORTH EAST

CARTOON BOOKS
ON FOOT & FINGER
ON MORE FEET & FINGERS
LAUGHS ALONG THE PENNINE WAY

*Also a full range of guidebooks
to walking, scrambling, ice-climbing,
rock climbing, and other adventurous
pursuits in Britain and abroad*

*Other guides are constantly being added to the Cicerone List.
Available from bookshops, outdoor equipment shops or direct (send for price list)
from CICERONE, 2 POLICE SQUARE, MILNTHORPE, CUMBRIA, LA7 7PY*

143

Printed by CARNMOR PRINT & DESIGN
95-97 LONDON ROAD, PRESTON, LANCASHIRE, UK.